Solving Business Problems

Using a Calculator

Sixth Edition

Mildred K. Polisky
Business Education Consultant
Formerly Instructor-Manager, Business Learning Center
Milwaukee Area Technical College
Milwaukee, Wisconsin

 **Glencoe McGraw-Hill**

New York, New York   Columbus, Ohio   Chicago, Illinois   Peoria, Illinois   Woodland Hills, California

Glencoe/McGraw-Hill

A Division of The **McGraw·Hill** *Companies*

Printed in the United States of America.

Send all inquiries to:
Glencoe/McGraw-Hill
21600 Oxnard Street
Woodland Hills, CA 91367-4906

ISBN-13: 978-0-07-830020-2   (Student Edition)
ISBN-10: 0-07-830020-7

ISBN-13: 978-0-07-830021-9   (Instructor Manual & Key)
ISBN-10: 0-07-830021-5

17   LCR   24 23 22

*The author dedicates this
book to her husband, Arnold,
their children, Beth and
Barry Reisig, and their
grandchildren, Adam and
Lauren.*

Solving Business Problems Using a Calculator

PREFACE

Solving Business Problems Using a Calculator follows current trends in office technology, teaches the touch method, explains common calculator features, and emphasizes business problem solving. In the sixth edition, the text's popular features have been maintained along with its concise explanations and emphasis on the use of the calculator as a problem-solving tool. Although specific calculators are mentioned in the text, any calculator with the same keys can be used. The applicable National Council of Teachers of Mathematics Standards and the American Mathematical Association of Two-Year Colleges Standards are used in the text.

ORGANIZATION

Solving Business Problems Using a Calculator is divided into six sections, comprising a total of 34 lessons. Each section has a Business Calculator Applications feature that parallels the applications used in that particular section and explains the use of a business calculator, the Texas Instruments BA-35 Solar Calculator. Lessons 8 through 34 explain how to use the calculator to solve everyday business and consumer problems. The business and consumer applications include payrolls, purchase orders, invoices, cash and trade discounts, calculating and verifying extensions, checking accounts, pricing, installment buying, proration, financial statement analysis, finance charges, allocation expenses and budgeting, and true annual interest rate.

REVIEWERS

Kim Belden
Daytona Beach Community College
Daytona Beach, Florida

Stephen J. Galambos
Philadelphia Job Corps Center
Philadelphia, Pennsylvania

Elizabeth Keller
South Hills Business School
State College, Pennsylvania

Louise P. Lochhead
Davis High School
Kaysville, Utah

Ginger Davis
Educational Consultant for Secondary
and Postsecondary
University Heights, Ohio

Karen D. Johnson
Ivy Tech State College
Muncie, Indiana

Carolyn S. Lewis
Center for Training in Business Industry
Lawrence, Kansas

Brenda A. B. Smith
State Technical Institute at Memphis
Memphis, Tennessee

CONTENTS

CONTENTS

CONTENTS

Common Calculator Features

Texas Instrument   TI-5660 FEATURES

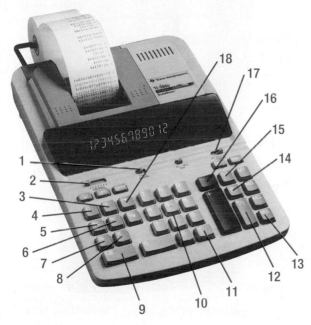

1. Rounding Switch
2. Decimal Selector
3. Divide Key
4. Clear Key (clears the display, the independent add register, any pending operation, and any error)
5. Change Sign Key
6. Equals Key
7. Percent Key
8. Multiply Key
9. Clear Entry Key (clears an entry)
10. Numerical Keys
11. Decimal Point Key
12. Total Key
13. Memory Keys
14. Subtotal Key
15. Grand Total Key (printer switch must be set to GT to activate a grand total)
16. Subtract Key
17. Off/On Key
18. Right Shift Key (removes the last digit entered in the display)

Texas Instrument BA-35 SOLAR FEATURES

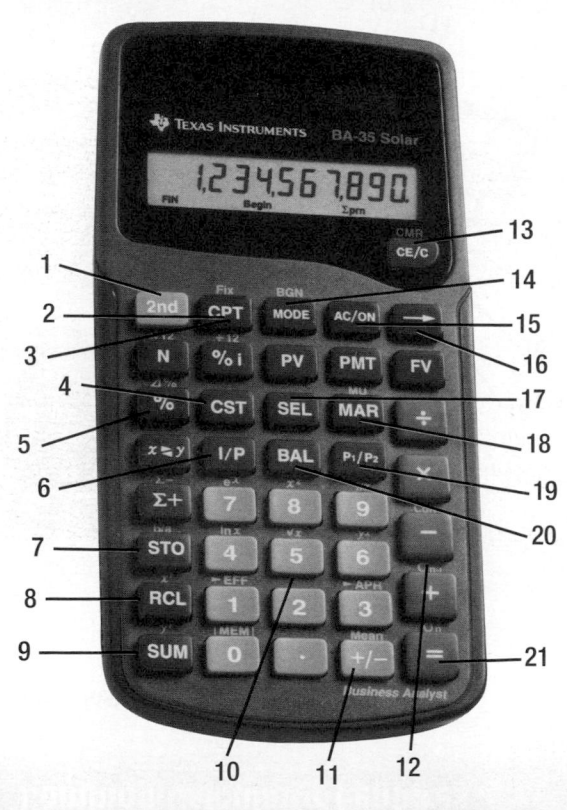

1. 2nd (2nd Function Key) (enables you to perform the second functions that are marked over some keys)
2. 2nd [FIX] (sets the number of decimal places)
3. CPT (Computation Key) (computes the unknown values for gross profit margin and markup problems)
4. CST (enters the cost)
5. Percent Key
6. I/P (Interest and Principal Key) (calculates the interest and principal portions of a single payment)
7. STO (Store Key) (stores the displayed numeric value)
8. RCL (recalls a value already entered)
9. SUM (adds the displayed value to the memory)

10. Numerical Keys
11. Change Sign Key
12. Operation Keys
13. Clear Entry/Clear Key
14. Mode Key (changes the calculator to the next mode in the sequence)
15. All Clear/On Key
16. Backspace Key (removes last digit entered)
17. SEL (enters the selling price)
18. MAR (enters the gross profit margin)
19. P1/P2 (enters a selected range of payments)
20. BAL (calculates the remaining loan balance [principal] after payment)
21. Equals Key

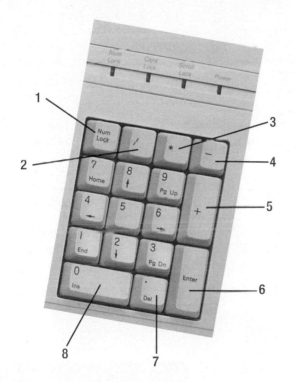

1. Number Lock Key (the numbers pressed appear on the screen)
2. Division Key
3. Multiplication Key
4. Subtraction Key
5. Addition Key
6. Enter Key (enters the information of the screen)
7. Delete Key
8. Insert Key (deletes previous copy as you type over it)

L E S S O N 1

THE HOME-ROW KEYS: 4 , 5 , 6

The home-row keys, 4 , 5 , and 6 , are the base position for your fingers on the keyboard. The other keys are found easily by reaching above or below the home row. The home-row keys often have a greater depression than the other keys. The 5 key might have a raised dot on it so that the user can find the home row by touch.

The touch system means that users do **not** look at the keys. Instead, they keep their eyes on the problem.

Your calculator may or may not accumulate addition on the screen.

TOUCH ADDITION OF WHOLE NUMBERS

Tape	Screen
0. T	0
4. +	4.
5. +	9.
6. +	15.
44. +	59.
45. +	104.
46. +	150.
55. +	205.
56. +	261.
456. +	717.
717. T *or* *	

If the addition does not accumulate on your tape model calculator, your answers will be like those shown on the tape above. If your display calculator accumulates addition on the screen, your answers will be like those shown on the right.

OBJECTIVES

- *Perform touch addition of whole numbers.*
- *Complete Progress Test 1 within 10 minutes and without errors.*

Home-row position

Demonstration Problem

```
      4
      5
      6
     44
     45
     46
     55
     56
    456
    717
```

Follow the steps at the right to work the demonstration problem. Enter the numbers into the calculator using the correct fingers and without looking at the keys.

The illustration on page 2 shows the position of the right hand on the home-row keys. Use the index finger on the [4] key, the middle finger on the [5] key, and the ring finger on the [6] key.

1. Clear the calculator by pressing the Total key, labeled [T] or [*] on the tape model. Use the Clear key, [C], on the screen or display model.

2. Set the calculator to add whole numbers by setting the Decimal Point Selector at zero. (See the instructions for your calculator.)

3. Curve the index, middle, and ring fingers over the [4], [5], and [6] keys.

4. Try to keep your eyes on the numbers in the problem as you add by touch.

5. Enter 4 on the keyboard with your index finger. Then add.

6. Add by pressing the Plus bar, [+], with your little finger.

7. Enter 5 with your middle finger and add with the [+] bar.

8. Enter 6 with your ring finger and add.

9. Enter 44 with your index finger and add.

10. Enter 45 with your index and middle fingers and add.

11. Enter 46 with your index and ring fingers and add.

12. Enter 55 with your middle finger and add.

13. Enter 56 with your middle and ring fingers and add.

14. Enter 456 and add.

15. Find the total. On the tape model, press the Total key. On the screen model, simply read the screen. Clear the screen with the Clear key, [C].

16. Repeat the problem until you get 717 for the total.

CHECKING TOUCH ADDITION.

Press the ☐4 , ☐5 , and ☐6 keys by touch as you enter the numbers in Problems A through J on the keyboard. After you add each problem, compare your total with the total given. Do not start a new problem until you have added the one before it correctly.

NOTE: If you press a wrong key as you are entering the numbers, you can clear the error from the keyboard **before** pressing the ☐+ bar by pressing the Clear Entry, ☐CE , the Clear Keyboard, ☐CK , or the Clear Display, ☐CD , key on your calculator. (See the instructions for your model if it has none of these keys.)

REMEMBER: Set your Decimal Point Selector at zero to add whole numbers.

A.	B.	C.	D.	E.
5	5	64	44	666
6	4	46	45	555
4	4	66	54	646
6	6	55	55	444
5	5	44	56	454
6	4	45	65	565
4	5	56	64	456
5	6	65	46	654
4	5	54	45	555
45	44	495	474	4,995

F.	G.	H.	I.	J.
444	666	454	66	556
555	44	565	444	44
666	55	446	55	5
546	45	456	6	45
456	555	45	45	66
544	54	65	4	465
466	56	555	456	564
645	66	664	65	655
556	654	56	656	6
4,878	2,195	3,306	1,797	2,406

THE HOME-ROW KEYS: 4 , 5 , 6

Use the touch system to add Problems 1 through 10. Use the appropriate fingers to enter the numbers on the keyboard. Do not look at the keys.

Record your answers to all problems on the numbered Answer Tabs at the back of the book. Remove the perforated Answer Tabs as you need them.

Remove the Answer Tab for Lesson 1 on the last page of the book and record your answers on the appropriate lines. The Answer Tabs are perforated for easy removal.

1.	2.	3.	4.	5.
4	4	65	654	56
5	44	454	5,544	454
6	6	55	456	55
4	56	564	6,546	5,564
4	65	44	645	65
5	5	6	6	445
6	54	665	45	654
5	55	545	445	5

6.	7.	8.	9.	10.
465	66	4,565	44	4
654	55	565	55	45
444	46	65	66	456
454	456	5	444	654
555	564	6	555	65
565	654	46	666	6
666	65	546	1,556	55
456	45	4,546	5,665	444

THE ZERO KEY: 0

The 0 key is pressed with the side of the right thumb. Check the addition of Problems K and L. Add Problems 11 through 18 and record your answers on the Answer Tab for Lesson 1.

K.	L.	11.	12.	13.
40	60	55	600	65
50	50	400	505	405
60	40	66	506	540
450	55	450	405	450
460	505	550	660	505
540	404	50	604	55
560	550	640	650	650
60	660	505	60	500
2,220	2,324			

14.	15.	16.	17.	18.
50	4,600	400	50	500
6	5,440	505	5	660
505	5,600	660	505	506
460	550	605	605	450
56	50	640	60	504
560	605	550	45	555
600	6,546	540	40	605
65	500	650	50	60

THE UPPER ROW OF KEYS: 7, 8, 9

Remember to keep your fingers positioned on the home-row keys, which are the base positions for your fingers on the keyboard. Then use the index finger to enter 7 on the keyboard, the middle finger to enter 8, and the ring finger to enter 9. Check the addition of Problems M and N. Add Problems 19 through 26 and record your answers on the Answer Tab for Lesson 1.

M.	N.	19.	20.	21.
47	59	47	580	90
58	69	58	75	700
69	48	69	890	670
96	47	57	700	690
85	57	58	950	745
74	68	59	570	89
78	95	69	86	498
89	84	78	805	99
596	527			

22.	23.	24.	25.	26.
49	458	45	789	458
444	95	56	987	95
657	88	67	860	488
660	866	78	950	466
560	90	89	640	90
900	776	98	480	776
88	75	87	690	75
770	405	76	670	405

THE LOWER ROW OF KEYS: 1 , 2 , 3

Use the index finger to enter 1 on the keyboard, the middle finger to enter 2, and the ring finger to enter 3. Check the addition of Problems O and P. Add Problems 27 through 34 and record your answers on the Answer Tab for Lesson 1.

O.	P.	27.	28.	29.
12	123	31	110	910
23	231	25	53	250
13	321	36	28	52
31	340	51	210	517
36	100	24	37	258
39	200	36	75	769
28	350	22	670	65
17	150	32	35	800
199	1,815			

30.	31.	32.	33.	34.
495	95	159	741	123
250	98	358	852	356
29	87	14	963	789
200	115	147	357	247
71	348	125	159	258
389	359	259	247	369
781	500	369	169	753
350	987	357	358	862

THE NUMERIC KEYBOARD

All the numeric keys, 0 through 9, are covered in Problems 35 through 44.

Record your answers for problems 35 through 46 on the Answer Tab for Lesson 1. Do not look at your keys. Use the touch system to enter the numbers.

After you complete Lesson 1, check with your instructor about taking Progress Test 1 on pages 218 and 219.

35.	36.	37.	38.	39.
300	390	986	650	350
490	170	315	303	20
2,300	96	547	621	755
250	59	770	954	9,630
60	907	322	809	876
199	301	25	704	53
360	375	989	911	96
246	733	730	527	250

40.	41.	42.	43.	44.
525	174	894	857	84
41	56	658	852	780
531	502	987	210	77
303	98	573	567	73
12	63	858	582	942
606	1,328	736	12	52
227	808	815	541	238
184	985	200	695	234

45. Communication   Explain how to use the touch system on the 10-key keyboard.

46. Communication   What is the function of the [CE] key?

L E S S O N 2

TOUCH ADDITION AND SUBTRACTION OF WHOLE NUMBERS

OBJECTIVES

- *Add and subtract whole numbers with positive or negative balances.*
- *Find subtotals and totals in addition and subtraction.*
- *Perform repeat addition and subtraction.*
- *Complete Progress Test 2 within 10 minutes and without errors.*

Addition and subtraction can be done within a single problem. Subtract numbers by pressing the Minus bar, $\boxed{-}$, with your little finger.

Demonstration Problem

$$\begin{array}{r} 485 \\ -365 \\ 589 \\ -350 \\ 775 \\ -980 \\ 150 \\ \underline{-123} \\ 181 \end{array}$$

1. Clear the calculator with the Clear key, $\boxed{C}$, $\boxed{CE/C}$, $\boxed{CK}$, or Total key, $\boxed{T}$.
2. Set the Decimal Point Selector at zero.
3. Use the touch method to enter all amounts.

Enter	Press	Tape	Screen
	$\boxed{T}$	0. T	0.
485	$\boxed{+}$	485. +	485.
365	$\boxed{-}$	365. −	120.
589	$\boxed{+}$	589. +	709.
350	$\boxed{-}$	350. −	359.
775	$\boxed{+}$	775. +	1,134.
980	$\boxed{-}$	980. −	154.
150	$\boxed{+}$	150. +	304.
123	$\boxed{-}$	123. −	181.
	$\boxed{T}$	181. T	

CHECKING TOUCH ADDITION AND SUBTRACTION.

Check Problems A through E. Add the numbers that are not preceded by a minus sign and subtract the numbers that are preceded by a minus sign. Do not begin a new problem until you have gotten the correct answer to the one before it.

POSITIVE BALANCES

Problems 1 through 5 have positive balances. That means that the total of the numbers added is greater than the total of the numbers subtracted.

Record your answers to Problems 1 through 5 on the Answer Tab for Lesson 2 at the back of the book.

A.	B.	C.	D.	E.
587	958	1,245	475	3,585
− 132	−570	−1,655	−198	−369
455	175	−1,075	346	−4,500
	563	5,440	−332	−3,500
		−600	705	9,875
		1,690	950	−5,000
		5,045	−158	6,936
			−767	497
			1,021	52,255
				40,000
				19,779

1.	2.	3.	4.	5.
648	901	747	3,950	1,918
− 375	−369	−589	−777	−5,575
	−675	653	1,275	−5,055
	575	−217	−2,500	−3,750
		−456	−369	−4,000
		909	−1,515	1,675
			2,580	2,990
			−2,600	19,975
				−3,600

NEGATIVE BALANCES

Problems 6 through 10 have negative balances. That means more was subtracted than was added. The result is a minus, or negative, number. Negative balances are shown with CR or a minus (−) sign. Some tapes print negative balances in red.

Demonstration Problem

$$525 - 750 = 225 \text{ CR} \quad or \quad -225$$

Enter	Press	Tape	Screen
	T	0. T	0.
525	+	525. +	525.
750	−	750. −	−225.
	T	−225. T	

Check Problem F and work Problems 6 through 16. Record your answers on the Answer Tab for Lesson 2.

F.	6.	7.	8.	9.	10.
257	498	125	159	320	824
−375	− 699	−660	−258	−282	−1,515
168		505	345	−415	235
−198		−225	−368	−150	990
−148				220	−3,200
				189	2,296
					−1,275
					−369

Problems 11 through 16 may have positive or negative balances.

11.	12.	13.	14.	15.	16.
857	475	−895	748	594	−123
−165	−585	256	−400	872	−234
375	−910	627	−446	−718	−345
−850	−885	−960	129	−674	−456
426	950	524	250	258	987
−105	546	650	−378	−738	776
			192	751	865
			−204	−370	654

SUBTOTALS

Tape calculators print a subtotal without clearing the amount from the calculator. Press the Subtotal key, $\boxed{S}$ or $\boxed{\diamond}$, with the little finger.

Some screen models show a running balance. This serves as a subtotal after each addition or subtraction.

REPEAT ADDITION OR SUBTRACTION

Press the $\boxed{+}$ or $\boxed{-}$ key to add or subtract repeated numbers. To total 30 + 30 − 25, just enter 30 one time. Press $\boxed{+}$ twice. Then subtract 25. Check instructions for your machine for repeat addition or subtraction.

Work the demonstration problem at the right. Check Problem G and work Problems 17 through 21. Record your answers on the Answer Tab for Lesson 2.

Demonstration Problem

Problem	Enter	Press	Tape	Screen
		$\boxed{T}$	0. T	0.
30	30	$\boxed{+}$	30. +	30.
30		$\boxed{+}$	30. +	60.
−25	25	$\boxed{-}$	25. −	35.
35	S	$\boxed{S}$	35. S	
193 S	193	$\boxed{+}$	193. +	228.
−45	45	$\boxed{-}$	45.	103.
−45		$\boxed{-}$	45. −	138.
138 T	T	$\boxed{T}$	138. T	

G.	17.	18.	19.	20.	21.
55	381	58	145	357	818
52	−228	−58	−275	357	650
52	−228	65	191	680	−853
159 S	S	S	S	S	S
−125	125	27	813	−369	212
−136	890	−39	−280	−120	−212
75	12	−92	280	−989	820
−27 T	T	T	T	T	T

Business Application

VERIFYING INVENTORY CARDS

Inventory cards are used to keep a record of merchandise in stock. *Quantities received* (Qty Rec) are added. *Quantities sold* (Qty Sold) are subtracted. The balance shows the items in stock on the date of each entry.

Many business records are prepared by one employee. They are verified and checked for accuracy by another person.

Check Problems H through N. Then verify and check the inventory cards in Problems 22 through 51. Record your answers for Problems 22 through 53 on the Answer Tab for Lesson 2.

1. To check an inventory card, find a subtotal to verify each balance.

2. Write a check (✓) beside correct balances.

3. Give correct balances for those that are incorrect.

INVENTORY CARD

Item Hand-held calculators

Supplier No. C-97-T

Aisle 7   Bin 3

Maximum 200   Minimum 60

Date	Quantity Received	Quantity Sold	Balance
1/20	200		200
1/22		47	153
1/28		55	98
2/2		38	66
2/9	150	35	181
2/11		60	121
2/16		58	63

H. ✓
I. ✓
J. ✓
K. 60
L. 175
M. 115
N. 57

	Enter	Press	Tape	Screen
		T	0. T	0.
	200	+	200. +	200.
		S	200. S	
	47	−	47. −	153.
		S	153. S	
	55	−	55. −	98.
		S	98. S	
	38	−	38. −	60.
		S	60. S	
	150	+	150. +	210.
	35	−	35. −	175.
		S	175. S	
	60	−	60. −	115.
		S	115. S	
	58	−	58. −	57.
		T	57. T	

INVENTORY CARD

Item <u>Calculator tape, 3 per pkg.</u>
Supplier No. <u>CT-97</u>
Aisle <u>8</u>　　Bin <u>2</u>
Maximum <u>250 pkg</u>.Minimum<u>75 pkg</u>.

Date	Quantity Received	Quantity Sold	Balance	
1/20	250		250	**22.**
1/22		75	175	**23.**
1/25		95	80	**24.**
2/2	150		230	**25.**
2/4		65	195	**26.**
2/9		98	103	**27.**
2/14	185	22	266	**28.**
2/17		110	156	**29.**
2/19		70	86	**30.**
2/20	200	50	236	**31.**

INVENTORY CARD

Item <u>Calculator tape, single</u>
Supplier No. <u>CT-101</u>
Aisle <u>8</u>　　Bin <u>1</u>
Maximum <u>2,500</u>　Minimum <u>500</u>

Date	Quantity Received	Quantity Sold	Balance	
1/20	2,500		2,500	**32.**
1/22		144	2,356	**33.**
1/24		288	2,068	**34.**
1/27		500	1,568	**35.**
2/4		576	1,001	**36.**
2/6		480	521	**37.**
2/11	2,000	150	2,362	**38.**
2/14		360	1,966	**39.**
2/18		288	1,678	**40.**
2/20		360	1,238	**41.**

INVENTORY CARD

Item <u>Desk calculators</u>
Supplier No. <u>C-101-M</u>
Aisle <u>7</u>　　Bin <u>1</u>
Maximum <u>100</u>　Minimum <u>25</u>

Date	Quantity Received	Quantity Sold	Balance	
1/20	100		100	**42.**
1/22		20	80	**43.**
1/24		32	57	**44.**
1/27		28	29	**45.**
1/31	75	30	74	**46.**
2/4		24	50	**47.**
2/6		24	8	**48.**
2/11	110	15	123	**49.**
2/14		20	103	**50.**
2/18		15	88	**51.**

52. Communication　Explain what *positive balance* means in a problem with plus and minus amounts?

53. Communication　Make up a problem that has a negative balance.

After you complete Lesson 2, check with your instructor about taking Progress Test 2 on pages 220 and 221.

LESSON 3

CROSSFOOTING

CROSSFOOTING

Business problems often require two sets of totals from the same numbers: one added down and one added across. This is called **crossfooting**. The sum of the column (down) totals equals the sum of the row (across) totals. This is a check on the accuracy of the **grand total**.

Work through the demonstration problem on the next page.

1. Clear all figures from the calculator.

2. Set the Decimal Point Selector at zero.

3. Add down each column and check your answers.

4. Add across each row and check your answers.

5. Add the column totals to get the grand total.

6. Add the row totals to check the grand total.

Demonstration Problem

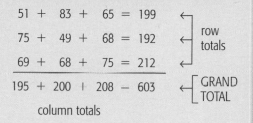

$$51 + 83 + 65 = 199 \leftarrow$$
$$75 + 49 + 68 = 192 \leftarrow \quad \text{row totals}$$
$$69 + 68 + 75 = 212 \leftarrow$$
$$195 + 200 + 208 = 603 \leftarrow \quad \text{GRAND TOTAL}$$

column totals

CHECKING CROSSFOOTING. Check Problem A. After you have gotten the correct answers, work Problems 1 through 8.

A.	9,999	+	3,412	+	8,916	+	10,003	=	**32,330**
	6,616	+	201	+	643	+	9,998	=	**17,458**
	8,903	+	6,201	+	1,009	+	730	=	**16,843**
	25,518	+	**9,814**	+	**10,568**	+	**20,731**	=	**66,631**

Record the answers to Problems 1 through 8 on the Answer Tab for Lesson 3.

7,710	+	6,243	+	18,891	+	3,112	=	_____ **5.**
1,186	+	10,999	+	2,347	+	6,820	=	_____ **6.**
6,401	+	7,789	+	642	+	8,102	=	_____ **7.**
1. _____	+	**2.** _____	+	**3.** _____	+	**4.** _____	−	_____ **8.**

Business Application 1

This report shows the amount of sales by four agents during the first six months of a year. Crossfoot this report. Write your answers on the Answer Tab for Lesson 3.

1. Find the agent totals: add down each column.

2. Find the monthly totals: add across each row.

3. Find the grand total: add the agent totals (Answers 9, 10, 11, and 12).

4. Check the grand total: add the monthly totals (Answers 13, 14, 15, 16, 17, and 18).

MONTHLY SALES BY AGENT

Month	Klaus	Guerra	Wong	Brown	Monthly Totals
January	$42,325	$33,105	$37,798	$40,095	_____ 13.
February	44,400	36,200	38,700	41,100	_____ 14.
March	47,750	39,275	39,950	43,100	_____ 15.
April	48,800	40,400	41,050	44,775	_____ 16.
May	48,200	42,575	39,775	42,395	_____ 17.
June	47,675	44,444	42,333	45,998	_____ 18.
Agent Totals	9. _____	10. _____	11. _____	12. _____	_____ 19.

Grand Total

Business Application 2

This table shows the college degrees granted in selected fields over a five-year period. Crossfoot this table. Write your answers on the Answer Tab for Lesson 3.

1. Find the year totals: add down each column.

2. Find the field totals: add across each row.

3. Find the grand total: add the year totals.

4. Check the grand total: add the field totals.

Write your answers for Problems 34 and 35 on the Answer Tab for Lesson 3.

COLLEGE DEGREES GRANTED IN SELECTED FIELDS

Field	Year					Field Totals
	1st	2nd	3rd	4th	5th	
Architecture	1,356	1,501	1,810	1,956	2,312	_____ 25.
Business	36,037	40,561	49,252	58,765	75,369	_____ 26.
Dentistry	2,501	3,199	3,333	3,269	3,750	_____ 27.
Education	45,452	57,659	81,257	80,101	85,231	_____ 28.
Engineering	31,246	32,589	36,707	37,795	42,442	_____ 29.
Law	13,412	9,225	9,654	11,999	14,752	_____ 30.
Medicine	5,621	7,165	7,704	7,437	8,734	_____ 31.
Nursing	4,272	4,425	5,660	7,998	11,821	_____ 32.
Year Totals	20. _____	21. _____	22. _____	23. _____	24. _____	_____ 33.

Grand Total

34. **Communication** In your own words, define *crossfooting*.

35. **Communication** Why is it important to check your answers in crossfooting?

L E S S O N 4

TOUCH ADDITION AND SUBTRACTION OF DOLLARS AND CENTS

THE ADD/MODE POSITION

The **Add/Mode** (+) position of the decimal selector saves time by marking two decimal points in each entry.

Enter 4 2 5 for $1.25.

Enter 1 2 5 0 0 for $125.00.

Demonstration Problem

$2.36
5.00
−1.25
3.49
−3.69
2.58
―――
$8.49

1. Clear all figures from the calculator.

2. Set the calculator in the Add/Mode (+) position. If the calculator does not have an Add/Mode position, set the Decimal Selector at two.

    a. If you use the Add/Mode position, enter all numbers to be added or subtracted. The machine will automatically mark two decimal places. To enter $2.36, press 2 3 6 . To enter $5.00, press 5 0 0 .

    b. If you set the Decimal Selector at two, press the Decimal Point key at the proper place. To enter $2.36, press 2 . 3 6 . To enter $5.00, press 5 . 0 0 .

Enter	Press	Tape	Screen
	T	0.00 T	0.
2.36	+	2.36 +	2.36
5.00	+	5.00 +	7.36
1.25	−	1.25 −	6.11
3.49	+	3.49 +	9.60
3.69	−	3.69 −	5.91
2.58	+	2.58 +	8.49
	T	8.49 T	

CHECKING ADDITION AND SUBTRACTION OF DOLLARS AND CENTS. Using the touch method, check the addition and subtraction in Problems A and B. Record your answers for Problems 1 through 8 on the Answer Tab for Lesson 4.

A.	B.	1.	2.	3.
$12.35	$5.65	$14.00	$86.13	$75.66
24.76	8.05	10.01	.57	13.50
−3.59	−5.64	82.22	−44.12	92.95
51.00	−9.87	61.50	50.05	−12.52
10.01	−5.21	57.50	−16.75	47.00
−8.68	3.00	60.40	23.45	93.99
$85.85	$−4.02	36.99	35.46	−18.75
		12.34	26.97	15.00

4.	5.	6.	7.	8.
$123.45	$4,005.00	$188.00	$3,160.00	$1,307.72
569.87	234.50	−205.00	2,125.45	5,015.05
−87.01	−975.68	117.72	5,205.13	7,133.70
754.53	357.98	543.28	−1,999.99	3,336.33
236.98	258.69	−765.89	1,070.00	1,511.25
−100.00	−2,000.00	500.00	3,050.15	−8,350.00
79.08	124.08	−255.16	−8,765.98	−4,000.00
35.00	−3,579.46	−987.65	4,446.46	9,150.00

Business Application 1

A deposit slip serves as a record of the amounts deposited in a bank account. To prepare a deposit slip, enter the total amount of paper money on the currency line and the total amount of change on the coin line. List the amount of each check separately. With this method, the total can be verified, and a check may be traced back to its deposit more easily.

Total the bank deposit slips shown at the right. Record your answers for Problems 9 and 10 on the Answer Tab for Lesson 4.

MILWAUKEE NATIONAL BANK
Milwaukee, Wisconsin

A.P. Distributors
312-312

Date _October 8_ 20 _ _

Currency	1,850	00
Coin	432	50
Checks:		
1.	765	89
2.	123	45
3.	500	00
4.	35	98
5.	15	75
6.	158	97
7.	246	80
8.	357	69
9.	98	98
TOTAL DEPOSIT ▶		

9.

MILWAUKEE NATIONAL BANK
Milwaukee, Wisconsin

A.P. Distributors
312-312

Date _October 15_ 20 _ _

Currency	1,500	00
Coin	357	75
Checks:		
1.	1,000	00
2.	357	99
3.	124	00
4.	75	98
5.	136	96
6.	248	97
7.	531	77
8.	258	07
9.	136	00
TOTAL DEPOSIT ▶		

10.

Business Application 2

A check register allows a depositor to keep track of the balance in an account. An account is opened with a deposit. Deposits are added to the balance. Each check is subtracted from the balance. Service charges, if any, are also subtracted. If all deposits and checks are recorded accurately, the depositor should know the correct balance.

Check the balances for Problems C and D. Then complete the balance column and write your answers on the Answer Tab for Lesson 4. Note that the account began with a zero balance.

After completing Lesson 4, check with your instructor about taking Progress Test 3 on pages 222 and 223.

Ask your instructor for Project 1.

CHECK NO.	DATE	CHECKS ISSUED TO OR DESCRIPTION OF DEPOSIT	AMOUNT OF CHECK		AMOUNT OF DEPOSIT		BALANCE		
	2/3	Deposit-paycheck			938	82	938	82	
							938	**82**	**C.**
101	2/3	Tusso Realty	550	00			550	00	
		rent					**388**	**82**	**D.**
102	2/5	Brown Discount	95	99			95	99	
		coat							**11.**
103	2/5	First State Bank	50	00			50	00	
		cash							**12.**
104	2/5	Quality Paints	34	67			34	67	
		paint							**13.**
105	2/8	Prime Oil Company	75	00			75	00	
		January gas bills							**14.**
106	2/8	Pacific Telephone	25	57			25	57	
		telephone							**15.**
	2/17	Deposit-paycheck			938	82	938	82	
									16.
107	2/18	First State Bank	150	00			150	00	
		car payment							**17.**
108	2/19	City Savings and Loan	100	00			100	00	
		savings							**18.**

5

ROUNDING AND ESTIMATING WITHOUT A CALCULATOR

ROUNDING

Calculated answers are sometimes rounded to make them easier to read and use. For instance, a manufacturing cost of $.27999 might be rounded to $.28.

People round to the degree of accuracy (or place value) they need. Amounts might be rounded to the nearest thousand, hundred, or hundredth (cent).

RULES FOR ROUNDING

Numbers can be rounded to different places (place-value positions). To round, look at the digit to the right of the place to be rounded.

1. If the digit to the right is 5 or more, add 1 to the rounded place and change the digits to the right to zeros.

2. If the digit to the right is 4 or less, the place being rounded remains the same. Then change all digits to the right to zeros.

3. The rules apply to decimals, too. Drop all zeros to the right of the decimal.

The place values of 13,745.1628 are shown here. Note that the place values to the right of the decimal point end with *ths*. Cents are made up of tenths and hundredths.

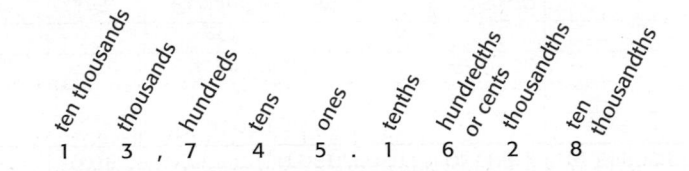

Demonstration Problems

Round 13,745 as indicated.

13,745 to the nearest thousand is 14,000

↑— 5 or more? Add 1 to the 3. Change digits to
the right to zeros.

13,745 to the nearest hundred is 13,700

↑—4 or less? Change digits to zeros.

Round 45.1628 as indicated.

45.1628 to the nearest tenth is 45.2 ___ ___ ___

↑—5 or more? Add 1. Drop digits.

$45.1628   to the
    nearest $45.16 ___ ___
↑—   cent

4 or less? Drop digits.

Remember that the place value position for both
hundredths and cents is two places to the right of
the decimal point.

Check Problems A through D and round Problems 1 through 24 as indicated. Write
your answers on the Answer Tab for Lesson 5.

A. Round to the nearest hundredth.
.1999 _____ .20_____

C. Round to the nearest cent.
$125.6999 ____ $125.70____

B. Round to the nearest thousandth.
.1568 _____ .157_____

D. Round to the nearest tenth.
13.4321 _____ 13.4_____

Round to the nearest hundredth.
1. 17.6583
2. 8.0019
3. 125.3548
4. .9994
5. 3.5199
6. 125.3541

Round to the nearest hundred.
13. 435.8749
14. 382.1094
15. 710.0099
16. 994.3675
17. 94.6481
18. 225.5329

Round to the nearest thousandth.
7. .9999
8. 1.8188
9. 21.6954
10. 35.3925
11. $.7549
12. $1.2999

Round to the nearest cent.
19. $.0999
20. $2.0192
21. $21.5953
22. $35.6667
23. $1.3999
24. $25.3333

ESTIMATING MULTIPLICATION AND DIVISION

To be sure answers make sense, estimate mentally before using a calculator. One way to estimate multiplication answers is to round numbers to the greatest nonzero place value. Multiply the nonzero digits in your head. Count the number of decimal places and place the decimal point.

Since there are several ways to arrive at an estimate, your estimate may not match exactly the estimate in the text. This does not mean that your estimate is incorrect. Check with your teacher or instructor to verify your method.

NOTE: $\approx$ means *is approximately equal to*.

Demonstration Problems

To estimate $4,658 \times 332$:
1. Round $5,\underline{000} \times 3\underline{00}$ 3. Count zeros. $1,\underline{500,000}$
2. Multiply $5 \times 3 = 15$ $4,658 \times 332 \approx$
   $1,500,000$

To estimate $465.8 \times .0322$:
1. Round $\underline{500} \times \underline{30}$ 3. Count zeros. $1\underline{500}$
2. Multiply $5 \times 3 = 15$ 4. Place the decimal: $15.\underline{00}$
   $465.8 \times .0322 \approx 15$

Select the best estimates. Do not use a calculator.

E. $300 \times 500 = 1,500$ *or* $150,000$?   **G.** $5,000 \times .10 = 500$ *or* $50,000$?
F. $50 \times 8 = 40$ *or* 400?   **H.** $6 \times .002 = 1.2$ *or* $.012$?

ANSWERS: **E.** 150,000;   **F.** 400;   **G.** 500;   **H.** .012

Solve these mentally.

I. 800×50 **K.** 70×20 **M.** $600,000 \times .05$
J. $9,000 \times .2$ **L.** $4,000 \times 3,000$ **N.** $500 \times .07$

ANSWERS: **I.** 40,000;   **J.** 1,800;   **K.** 1,400;   **L.** 12,000,000;   **M.** 30,000;   **N.** 35

Select the best estimate. Do not use a calculator. Record your answers on the Answer Tab for Lesson 5.

		a.	**b.**	**c.**	**d.**
25.	195×222	400	4,000	40,000	400,000
26.	$3,591 \times 43$	1,600	16,000	160,000	1,600,000
27.	$.246 \times 1,936$	40	400	4,000	40,000
28.	$3,246 \times .088$	2.7	27	270	2,700
29.	127×398	4,000	40,000	400,000	4,000,000
30.	$875 \times .0565$	5.4	54	540	5,400
31.	$1,734 \times 587$	12,000	120,000	1,200,000	12,000,000
32.	$97,482 \times .1481$	10	100	1,000	10,000
33.	19.765×2.12	.4	4	40	400
34.	$68 \times .0055$	.042	.42	4.2	42

Estimates should be quick. You want to know only the approximate size of the answer. To estimate division answers, just round and divide.

Demonstration Problems

To estimate 19,980 ÷ 375:

1. Round 20,000 ÷ 400
2. Divide

$$\begin{array}{r} 50 \\ 400\overline{)20,000} \end{array}$$

19,980 ÷ 375 ≈ 50

When dividing by a decimal, the answer will be larger than the dividend.

To estimate 28.7 ÷ .055:

1. Round 30 ÷ .06
2. Divide

$$\begin{array}{r} 5\ 00 \\ \times 0\ 6.\overline{)3\ 0 \times 0\ 0.} \end{array}$$

28.7 ÷ .055 ≈ 500

After you complete Lesson 5, check with your instructor about taking Progress Test 4 on pages 224 and 225.

Select the best answer. Do not use a calculator.

O. 70,000 ÷ 500 = 140 *or* 1,400?　　**Q.** 600 ÷ .06 = 1,000 *or* 10,000?
P. 9,000 ÷ 200 = 45 *or* 450?　　　　**R.** 800 ÷ .2 = 400 *or* 4,000?

ANSWERS: **O.** 140;　**P.** 45;　**Q.** 10,000;　**R.** 4,000

Solve mentally.

S. 200 ÷ 40　　　　**U.** 6,000 ÷ 30　　　　**W.** 20,000 ÷ 500
T. 30 ÷ .03　　　　**V.** 8 ÷ .04　　　　　**X.** 400 ÷ 8,000

ANSWERS: **S.** 5;　**T.** 1,000;　**U.** 200;　**V.** 200;　**W.** 40;　**X.** .05

Select the best estimate. Do not use a calculator. Record your answers on the Answer Tab for Lesson 5.

#	Problem	a.	b.	c.	d.
35.	72,560 ÷ 485	a. 14	b. 140	c. 1,400	d. 14,000
36.	68,245 ÷ 325	a. 2	b. 20	c. 200	d. 2,000
37.	925 ÷ 289	a. .3	b. 3	c. 30	d. 300
38.	17,897 ÷ 3,124	a. 6	b. 60	c. 600	d. 6,000
39.	428 ÷ 8,765	a. .005	b. .05	c. .5	d. 5
40.	57 ÷ .08	a. .7	b. 7	c. 70	d. 700
41.	36,975 ÷ 487	a. 80	b. 800	c. 8,000	d. 80,000
42.	908 ÷ .25	a. 3	b. 30	c. 300	d. 3,000
43.	12,975 ÷ 6,435	a. .2	b. 2	c. 20	d. 200
44.	851 ÷ .17	a. 4,500	b. 45,000	c. 450,000	d. 4,500,000

6

MULTIPLICATION

OBJECTIVES

- *Multiply whole numbers.*
- *Multiply decimal numbers.*
- *Estimate answers in multiplication.*

MULTIPLICATION OF WHOLE NUMBERS

Multiplication is a very fast and simple process with all electronic calculators.

Demonstration Problem

$$33 \times 28 = 924$$

An estimate for the above problem would be

$$30 \times 30 = 900$$

This estimate tells you that the answer 924 is reasonable. Estimate before multiplying with a calculator.

Only two operating steps are required for multiplication.

1. Enter the first factor and press the Multiplication key, $\boxed{\times}$.

2. Enter the second factor and press the Equals key, $\boxed{=}$.

(If your machine has the plus sign and equals sign on one key, $\boxed{\pm}$, use that key to get the *product*.) The answer (the product) is then printed on the tape or registered on the screen.

Work the demonstration problem as follows.

1. Clear all figures from the calculator.

2. Set the Decimal Point Selector at zero.

Enter	Press	Tape	Screen
	$\boxed{T}$	0. T	0.
33	$\boxed{\times}$	33. ×	33.
28	$\boxed{=}$	28. =	28.
		924.	924.

Check Problems A and B before completing Problems 1 through 17.

First estimate each answer. Then set the Decimal Point Selector at zero and work each problem on the calculator. The calculated answer should be reasonably close to your estimate.

AN ESTIMATING HINT

Note in Problem B that both tens digits are 5 or greater. Usually, a multiplication estimate will be close if one factor is rounded *up* and one is rounded *down* or one remains the same.

Demonstration Problem

Estimate the product of 150 × 250.

150 is rounded *up* to 200
250 is rounded *down* to 200
200 × 200 = 40,000 (estimate)
150 × 250 = 37,500 (answer)

Record your answers on the Answer Tab for Lesson 6.

Estimate answers first. See how close you can get to the product.

	Factor		Factor	Your Estimate	Calculator's Product
A.	64	×	36	2,400	2,304
B.	575	×	658	360,000	378,350
1.	654	×	72		
2.	325	×	313		
3.	1,728	×	729		
4.	249	×	9		
5.	756	×	360		
6.	6,423	×	601		
7.	10,092	×	21		
8.	8,009	×	994		
9.	3,421	×	656		
10.	77	×	44		
11.	3,023	×	212		
12.	4,513	×	333		
13.	6,502	×	208		
14.	7,788	×	1,009		
15.	11,453	×	2,003		
16.	352	×	25		
17.	24	×	19		

MULTIPLICATION WITH DOLLARS AND CENTS

Most electronic calculators have a floating decimal. That means the calculator automatically computes where the decimal point should go in the answer.

THE ROUND SWITCH.   If the calculator has a Round switch, set it in the five/four position. This will round the answer to the place set by the Decimal Point Selector. To get answers to the nearest cent, set the Decimal Point Selector at two and the Round switch in the five/four position.

If there is no Round switch, set the Decimal Point Selector at three and round mentally to the nearest cent.

Throughout this book, if your calculator does not have a Decimal Point Selector, the floating decimal point will set the decimal. Then mentally round the answer to the required number of decimal places.

Demonstration Problem

$$\$24.97 \times 3.75 = 93.6375 \text{ or } \$93.64 \text{ (rounded to the nearest cent)}$$

1. Estimate the answer. Estimate 24.97×3.75 as 20×4. The answer is about 80.
2. Set the Decimal Point Selector at two.
3. Set the Round switch in the five/four position. If there is no Round switch, set the Decimal Point Selector at three and round mentally to the nearest cent. (Check the calculator instructions for the round capacity.)
4. Remember to press the Decimal Point key, ⬚ , in the correct places.
5. Clear the machine.

Enter	Press	Tape	Screen
	T	0.00 T	0.
24.97	×	24.97 ×	24.97
3.75	=	3.75 =	3.75
		93.64	93.64 *or*
			93.6375*

*To round the answer to the nearest cent, round the cents digit to 4 because the digit to the right of the cents is 7.

6. Compare your estimate and the calculator answer. The answer is reasonably close to the estimate.

Estimate your answer first. Then set the Decimal Point Selector at two and the Round switch in the five/four position for Problem C and Problems 18 through 25.

Set your calculator for a four-decimal-place answer in Problem D and Problems 26 through 34.

Check Problems C and D before completing the remaining problems. Estimate the answers and then use the calculator to find the products.

Record your answers on the Answer Tab for Lesson 6.

	Factor		Factor	Your Estimate	Calculator's Product
C.	$1.98	×	12	$20.00	$23.76
18.	$27.99	×	36		
19.	$35.99	×	48		
20.	$18.88	×	54		
21.	$19.95	×	103		
22.	$2.495	×	26		
23.	$14.99	×	7.5		
24.	$17.98	×	4.25		
25.	$279.95	×	12.33		
D.	36.25	×	12.955	400	469.6188
26.	18.875	×	13.75		
27.	20.667	×	8.25		
28.	63.333	×	71.125		
29.	44.625	×	19.375		
30.	19.983	×	11.22		
31.	16.595	×	11.75		
32.	12.559	×	35.125		
33.	28.333	×	31.625		
34.	52.825	×	98.333		

Business Application

An **invoice** is a complete listing of the quantity and price of items sold to the purchaser. Most invoices have at least four columns: quantity, description, unit price, and amount. Multiply each quantity by its unit price to get the **amount,** or extension. Then add the amounts to find the total of the invoice.

Demonstration Problem

24 dozen tennis ball cans at $23.99 per dozen

Estimate: $20 \times 30 = 600$

$24 \times \$23.99 = \$575.76$

Compared to the estimate, the answer is reasonable.

Estimate. Then complete the invoice on this page. Set the Decimal Point Selector at two and the Round switch in the five/four position. Write your answers on the Answer Tab for Lesson 6.

Check the demonstration problem and Problem E before completing Problems 35 through 41.

A.P. DISTRIBUTORS
11122 Glendale Road
Milwaukee, WI 53201

Invoice No. 13579

Date 2/2/- -

Terms Net 7 days

Sold to G. B. Sports Co.
3452 Landing Lane
Green Bay, WI 54301

Quantity	Description	Unit Price	Extension	
18	Tennis rackets	$39.75 ea	**$ 715.50**	E.
36	Basketballs	$27.35 ea	$_____	35.
12	Basketball backboard sets	$45.88 ea	$_____	36.
25	6-qt picnic lunch totes	$ 9.25 ea	$_____	37.
15	Hibachi grills	$17.36 ea	$_____	38.
100 bags	20-lb charcoal briquets	$ 5.39 ea	$_____	39.
18	Sleeping bags	$29.97 ea	$_____	40.
	TOTAL		$_____	41.

EXTENDING INVOICES

Finding the amounts, or extensions, and the total is called **extending an invoice.** Estimate. Then complete the extensions and total for the invoice to the right. Write your answers on the Answer Tab for Lesson 6.

Round all answers to the nearest cent. Set your Decimal Point Selector at two and the Round switch in the five/four position.

Check Problem F before completing the rest of the invoice.

NOTE: A unit price of $\$.07\frac{1}{4}$ is entered as .0725. A unit price of $\$.07\frac{1}{2}$ becomes .075.

Write your answers for Problems 49 through 51 on the Answer Tab for Lesson 6.

WELCO DISTRIBUTORS
11122 Glendale Road
Milwaukee, WI 53201

Invoice No. 8-1451

Date 8/1/- -

Terms Net 7 days

Sold to   Discount Stationery
530 Milwaukee Street
Sheboygan, WI 53081

Quantity	Description	Unit Price	Extension	
1,500	Pencils No. 200	$\$.07\frac{1}{4}$ each	**$108.75**	F.
375	Pencils No. 250	$\$.07\frac{1}{2}$ each	$_____	42.
75	Felt pens	$\$.35\frac{1}{2}$ each	$_____	43.
175	Ruled pads $8\frac{1}{2}$ x 11	$\$.23\frac{1}{4}$ each	$_____	44.
175	Pencil and ink erasers	$\$.09\frac{1}{4}$ each	$_____	45.
75	12-in. rulers	$\$.17\frac{1}{2}$ each	$_____	46.
75	Marking pens	$\$.47\frac{1}{2}$ each	$_____	47.
		TOTAL	$_____	48.

49. Communication   What is a factor?

50. Communication   Explain why it is important to estimate your answers.

51. Communication   What is a floating decimal on an electronic calculator?

LESSON 7

DIVISION

DIVISION OF WHOLE NUMBERS

Division, like multiplication, is a very fast and simple process with all electronic calculators.

Demonstration Problem

$$1,740 \div 12 = 145$$

An estimate for the above problem would be

$$2,000 \div 10 = 200$$

This estimate tells you that the answer 145 is reasonable. Estimate before dividing with a calculator.

Only two operating steps are required for division.

1. Enter the first amount (the dividend) and press the Division key, ÷ .

2. Enter the second amount (the divisor) and press the Equals key, = .
   The answer (the quotient) is then printed on the tape or displayed on the screen.

Complete the demonstration problem as follows.

1. Clear all figures from the calculator.

2. Set the Decimal Point Selector at zero.

3. Solve.

Enter	Press	Tape	Screen
	T	0. T	0.
1,740	+	1,740. ÷	1,740.
12	=	12. =	12.
		145.	145.

CHECKING THE DIVISION OF WHOLE NUMBERS AND ESTIMATING ANSWERS MENTALLY.

Check Problems A and B and the estimated answers. Complete Problems 1 through 15. Estimate your answers first. Then use the touch method for entering the dividend and divisor in the calculator.

Record your answers on the Answer Tab for Lesson 7.

One way to estimate a division problem is to round the divisor to its greatest place-value position. Do not change 1-digit divisors. Round the dividend so it is a multiple of the divisor.

	Dividend		Divisor		Estimate	Quotient
A.	168	÷	12	=	$170 \div 10 = 17$	14
B.	1,794	÷	39	=	$2,000 \div 40 = 50$	46
1.	35,770	÷	365	—		
2.	195,468	÷	546	=		
3.	1,578,528	÷	1,827	=		
4.	624	÷	48	=		
5.	3,996	÷	108	=		
6.	11,520	÷	256	=		
7.	169,568	÷	224	=		
8.	1,172,540	÷	2,549	=		
9.	4,405,815	÷	5,153	=		
10.	724,427	÷	5,987	=		
11.	106,964	÷	374	=		
12.	2,496	÷	64	=		
13.	27,225	÷	275	=		
14.	1,536	÷	12	=		
15.	11,433	÷	111	=		

DIVISION OF WHOLE NUMBERS WITH REMAINDERS

Calculators show remainders as decimal fractions. In the demonstration problem shown at the right, 157 ÷ 12, the number of decimal places appearing in the quotient depends on the decimal setting.

In calculators that do not have a Decimal Point Selector, the answer is carried out as far as the number of digits the screen contains. An eight-digit display screen would show 13.083333.

Before doing Problems 16 through 24, check the demonstration problem at the different decimal settings. Then set the Decimal Point Selector at two and the Round switch in the five/four position for answers with two decimal places. Estimate your answers first. Record answers on the Answer Tab for Lesson 7.

Demonstration Problem

Estimate: 150 ÷ 10 = 15

Decimal Setting	Dividend	Divisor	Quotient
0	157 ÷	12	= 13.
2	157 ÷	12	= 13.08
4	157 ÷	12	= 13.0833
6	157 ÷	12	= 13.083333

Compared to the estimate, the answer 13, is reasonable.

	Dividend	Divisor	Quotient
16.	227 ÷	15	= _____
17.	287 ÷	12	= _____
18.	1,777 ÷	25	= _____
19.	8,334 ÷	124	= _____
20.	15,789 ÷	360	= _____
21.	5,600 ÷	53	= _____
22.	5,769 ÷	33	= _____
23.	12,365 ÷	24	= _____
24.	3,798 ÷	24	= _____

Business Application

Salaries are often stated as yearly figures, but people are paid more often than once a year. To find the gross amount of one paycheck, divide the annual salary by the number of paychecks in a year.

Estimate. Then solve Problems 25 through 30. Round your answers to the nearest cent (two decimal places). Record your answers on the Answer Tab for Lesson 7.

DIVISION OF DECIMALS

Divide decimals as you would whole numbers. Be sure to press the decimal key in the right place. Set the Round switch for the answer needed.

Demonstration Problem

$1,891.4 \div 5.1875 =$

Estimate: $2,000 \div 5 = 400$

$1,891.4 \div 5.1875 = 364.6072289$

The answer is reasonable.

	Annual Salary	Number of Paychecks	Amount of Each Paycheck
25.	$32,875	52	$ _____
26.	$34,450	52	$ _____
27.	$39,975	26	$ _____
28.	$41,845	24	$ _____
29.	$35,300	24	$ _____
30.	$38,500	12	$ _____

In the division of 1,891.4 by 5.1875, the answer is automatically printed or displayed as shown below, with certain decimal place settings.

364.6	with a one-place decimal setting
364.61	with a two-place decimal setting
364.607	with a three-place decimal setting
364.6072	with a four-place decimal setting

Without a Decimal Point Selector, your answer would be 364.6072289, as shown in the demonstration problem. To arrive at the answers shown for specific decimal place settings, round the answer to the nearest tenth for a one-place setting, to the nearest hundredth for a two-place setting, to the nearest thousandth for a three-place setting, and to the nearest ten-thousandth for a four-place setting.

CHECKING DECIMAL DIVISION AND ROUNDING MENTALLY.

Set your calculator for a four-place decimal answer with the Round switch in the five/four position. There are two columns for your answers in Problems 31 through 43. The first column is for the four-decimal-place answer. The next column is for the answer rounded to three places.

Check Problems C and D before you continue with the remaining problems. Estimate your answers first. Then record your answers on the Answer Tab for Lesson 7.

	Dividend		Divisor		Four-Decimal-Place Answer	Quotient Rounded to Three Places
C.	1,891.3	÷	5.1875	=	364.5880	364.588
D.	896.05	÷	28.333	=	31.6257	31.626
31.	75.9167	÷	9.937	=		
32.	102.625	÷	5.123	=		
33.	217.142	÷	42.5	=		
34.	49.444	÷	7.75	=		
35.	112.0833	÷	24.87	=		
36.	5,194.5	÷	98.333	=		
37.	19.3758	÷	9.7778	=		
38.	5,423.1	÷	105.432	=		
39.	32.875	÷	4.333	=		
40.	357.319	÷	12.6667	=		
41.	84.857	÷	7.142	=		
42.	72.285	÷	11.3	=		
43.	9.5667	÷	18.7	=		

First, estimate your answers.

Set your calculator for a five-decimal-place answer in Problems 44 through 60. The second answer column is for the quotient rounded to four places.

Remember to record your answers on the Answer Tab for Lesson 7.

	Dividend		Divisor		Five-Decimal-Place Answer	Quotient Rounded to Four Places
44.	46.5714	÷	5.1	=		
45.	1,678.571	÷	101.5	=		
46.	428.6	:	502.625	=		
47.	117.8462	÷	13.125	=		
48.	63.1243	÷	5.4	=		
49.	84.1015	÷	14.1	=		
50.	12.1363	÷	24	=		
51.	360.105	÷	179	=		
52.	149.149	÷	280	=		
53.	147.121	÷	12	=		
54.	678.333	÷	125.2	=		
55.	259.5	÷	13	=		
56.	62.71	÷	7.1	=		
57.	49.003	÷	6.98	=		
58.	248.7	÷	12.2	=		
59.	7,035.3	÷	507.1	=		
60.	18.5	÷	9.1251	=		

Keypad Introduction

In each section of this text, there will be a two-page calculator feature based on the (Texas Instrument) BA-35 Solar calculator. You can use the TI BA-35 Solar calculator to compute all arithmetic problems throughout the text.

In this two-page feature, you will become familiar with the keypad on the TI BA-35 Solar calculator. The home-row, upper-row, and lower-row keys are in the same position on all 10-key calculators.

The **All Clear/ON** key AC/ON turns on the TI BA-35 Solar calculator. It also clears the display and all entries stored in memory. It is located on the top row of the keypad.

On the TI BA-35 Solar calculator, the **display** is located below the solar panel. The display shows a maximum of 10 digits, a decimal point, names of certain modes or functions in use, an ERROR indicator, and negative numbers. The **Change Sign** key +/− changes the sign of the number in the display. It is located next to the decimal key. To make a negative number positive or to make a positive number negative, press +/− .

Below the display, at the right, is the **Clear Entry/Clear** key CE/C . It clears a numerical entry when pressed once. To begin a new calculation, clear all operations by pressing CE/C twice.

A **function** is a mathematical relationship where one element in one set is paired with exactly one element of a second set.

Exercises

Write your response to each question on a separate piece of paper.

1. If 36 is in the display and you press $\boxed{+/-}$, what is in the display now?

2. What key clears the display and memory?

3. Name the three modes on the TI BA-35 Solar calculator.

4. Explain how the MODE key works.

5. What is the second function key?

6. What is the purpose of $\boxed{CE/C}$?

7. Enter 3625. Press the backspace key once. What is on the display now?

8. Explain what happens when you press $\boxed{2nd}$ [fix] $\boxed{.}$.

Notice the letters on and above certain keys. These letters represent functions. For calculator use, the functions *above* the keys are called *second* functions. The **Second Function** key $\boxed{2nd}$ allows you to perform the *second* functions. These keys will be explained as necessary in later sections. If you accidentally press $\boxed{2nd}$, press it again to cancel. The $\boxed{2nd}$ key is located on the top row of the keypad.

The last three keys and the second function above zero on the left-hand side of the keypad are memory keys. You should recognize the decimal point key, the operation keys, and the equals sign key. Any keys not discussed on this page are function keys.

The **MODE** key changes the calculator to the next mode. There are three modes—statistics, financial, and profit margin. In this text, only the last two will be used. FIN (financial) and STAT (statistics) are displayed in the lower left-hand corner of the display. Profit margin does not appear on the display. You can do operations in any mode. To choose a particular mode, press $\boxed{MODE}$ repeatedly until the appropriate mode is displayed. The $\boxed{MODE}$ key is located on the top row of the keypad.

Below the $\boxed{CE/C}$ is the **Backspac**e key $\boxed{\rightarrow}$. This key removes the last entry from the display. You can correct an error without clearing the display and starting again. The $\boxed{\rightarrow}$ is located on the top row of the keypad.

Practice Test 1

Problems 1 through 35 are a review of Lessons 1 through 7.

Remember to estimate all answers.

For Problems 1 through 4, set your calculator to Add/Mode. If it does not have Add/Mode, set the Decimal Point Selector at two.

Record your answers on the Answer Tab for Practice Test 1 at the back of the book.

1.	2.	3.	4.
$ .59	$2.98	$15.98	$59.98
1.00	2.40	−8.88	5.95
.95	1.98	−15.99	12.50
3.69	8.00	17.00	2.85
1.99	6.99	21.98	−25.00
4.59	6.98	9.00	7.50
1.19	24.98	1.00	−89.95
.27	12.99	−8.95	13.50
2.25	12.50	S	S
.29	.96	21.98	−13.99
.85	5.75	−18.00	3.99
1.09	5.75	−12.50	−7.57
.56	2.39	.79	3.99
.57	4.00	6.99	−11.50
1.25	12.99	24.98	29.50
T	T	T	T

Crossfoot Problems 5 through 18. Be sure to check your totals down and across.

Set the Decimal Point Selector at zero.

Record your answers on the Answer Tab for Practice Test 1.

6,352 +	5,181 +	8,110 +	3,233 +	9,302 =	_____ 10.
27,731 +	14,566 +	15,225 +	33,609 +	103,279 =	_____ 11.
5,297 +	3,990 +	3,427 +	5,315 +	3,478 =	_____ 12.
64,536 +	35,452 +	70,971 +	91,711 +	111,433 =	_____ 13.
25,642 +	22,985 +	33,088 +	36,579 +	42,227 =	_____ 14.
12,314 +	10,226 +	9,413 +	12,999 +	14,157 =	_____ 15.
6,521 +	7,506 +	7,740 +	7,437 +	8,748 =	_____ 16.
3,922 +	5,424 +	6,666 +	8,987 +	11,222 =	_____ 17.
					_____ 18.
5.	6.	7.	8.	9.	

Do not use your calculator for Problems 19 through 23.

For Problems 24 through 26, estimate the answers first. Then use the calculator for the actual numbers. Round to two decimal places.

Record your answers on the Answer Tab for Practice Test 1.

19. Round to the nearest ten: 2,859 _____   1,111 _____

20. Round to the nearest thousand: 9,852 _____   3,333 _____

21. Round to the nearest tenth: 4.2537 _____   3.6363 _____

22. Round to the nearest hundredth: 4.2538 _____   3.6366 _____

23. Round to the nearest cent: $9.999 _____ $10.275 _____

			Estimate	**Actual**
24. 466	×	124	= _____	_____
25. $9,950	÷	52	= _____	_____
26. 119	×	265	= _____	_____

Record your answers for Problems 27 through 35 with two decimal places. Record your answers to Problems 27 through 48 on the Answer Tab for Practice Test 1.

After you have completed Practice Test 1, check with your instructor about taking Test 1.

27. $19.95 × 2.625 = _____

28. 6,667 ÷ 267 = _____

29. $9,995 ÷ 52 = _____

30. 349 × .75 = _____

31. $279.50 × 18.76 = _____

32. 193,437 ÷ 369 = _____

33. $18,888.75 ÷ 362.2 = _____

34. $18,905 ÷ 236 = _____

35. 34.83 × 2.625 = _____

Name the place-value positions for each digit in 24,836.9715.
36. 4   **37.** 3   **38.** 9   **39.** 7   **40.** 1   **41.** 5

Round 24,836.9715 to the nearest place-value position listed below.
42. ten thousand   **43.** one   **44.** tenth   **45.** thousandth

46. State another name for the place-value position of cents.

47. Communication   Explain why it is important to estimate answers before using a calculator.

L E S S O N 8

CONSTANT MULTIPLICATION AND DIVISION

OBJECTIVES
- *Multiply with a constant factor.*
- *Divide with a constant divisor.*

A number that is repeated in a series of multiplication problems is called a **constant factor**. Multiplication with a constant factor is called **constant multiplication**.

Demonstration Problem

Hourly Rate		Hours Worked		Total Pay
$3.96	×	8	=	$ 31.68
$3.96	×	16	=	$ 63.36
$3.96	×	32	=	$126.72
$3.96	×	37.5	=	$148.50

1. Set the Decimal Point Selector at two.
2. Set the Round switch in the five/four position.
3. Set the calculator in the Constant Operation mode. (See the instruction manual for your particular calculator.)

Enter	Press	Tape	Screen	
	T	0.00 T	0.	
3.96	×	3.96 ×	3.96	
8	=	8.00 =	8.	Estimate: 4 × 8 = 32
		31.68	31.68	✓ Reasonable
16	=	16.00 =	16.	Estimate: 4 × 16 = 64
		63.36	63.36	✓ Reasonable
32	=	32.00 =	32.	Estimate: 4 × 30 = 120
		126.72	126.72	✓ Reasonable
37.5	=	37.50 =	37.5	Estimate: 4 × 40 = 160
		148.50	148.50	✓ Reasonable

Most calculators have a Constant Operation mode, that allows you to enter the first number of a multiplication problem as a constant factor. The constant factor has to be entered only once to solve problems involving a constant.

Some calculators have a Constant Operation switch or a Constant key, K. Many calculators have an automatic constant register, that holds the first number in multiplication as the constant number. Check the instruction manual for your calculator. If it has an automatic constant register, remember to enter the constant factor first.

Check the answers to Problems A and B before solving Problems 1 through 35 on pages 48–49.

Compared to the estimate, the answers are reasonable.

A. $4.12 per hour × 16 hours   = $ 65.92
$4.12 per hour × 24 hours   = $ 98.88
$4.12 per hour × 28.75 hours = $118.45
$4.12 per hour × 32.25 hours = $132.87

B. 20.75 dozen × $12.25 per dozen = $ 254.19
 13   dozen × $12.25 per dozen = $ 159.25
 27   dozen × $12.25 per dozen = $ 330.75
 18.5 dozen × $12.25 per dozen = $ 226.63
 8.25 dozen × $12.25 per dozen = $ 101.06

Did you remember to use $12.25 as the constant in Problem B and to enter it first? In multiplication, the constant factor must always be entered **first,** even though it is the second factor in the problem. If you did not enter $12.25 first in Problem B, repeat that problem before continuing to the next page.

Estimate. Then work Problems 1 through 35. Round all answers, that are money amounts, to two decimal places.

Note the demonstration problems on the left side of page 46. Check those answers before completing Problems 1 through 35.

Remember that the constant factor must always be entered **first** if your calculator has an automatic constant register.

Record your answers on the Answer Tab for Lesson 8.

	Hourly Rate		Hours Worked		Total Pay
1.	$4.85	×	8	=	$ _____
2.	$4.85	×	12	=	$ _____
3.	$4.85	×	32	=	$ _____
4.	$4.85	×	36	=	$ _____
5.	$5.97	×	40	=	$ _____
6.	$5.97	×	39	=	$ _____
7.	$5.97	×	38	=	$ _____
8.	$5.97	×	36	=	$ _____
9.	$5.97	×	37	=	$ _____
10.	$6.625	×	37	=	$ _____
11.	$6.625	×	32.5	=	$ _____
12.	$6.625	×	38.25	=	$ _____
13.	$6.625	×	34.75	=	$ _____
14.	$6.625	×	40	=	$ _____
15.	$8.00	×	35	=	$ _____
16.	$8.00	×	37.5	=	$ _____
17.	$8.00	×	40	=	$ _____

Demonstration Problems

$12 \times 12 = 144$
$12 \times 20 = 240$ } Enter 12 $\boxed{\times}$ first
$12 \times 36 = 432$

Estimate 432×18 as $400 \times 20 = 8,000$.
Compared to the estimate, 7,776 is reasonable.

$432 \times 18 = 7,776$
$546 \times 18 = 9,828$ } Enter 18 $\boxed{\times}$ first
$120 \times 18 = 2,160$

	Amount of Each Paycheck		Number of Paychecks		Annual Salary
18.	$ 700.00	×	26	= $	_____
19.	$ 981.00	×	26	= $	_____
20.	$1,053.08	×	26	= $	_____
21.	$ 776.00	×	26	= $	_____
22.	$ 753.90	×	26	= $	_____
23.	$ 853.84	×	26	= $	_____
24.	$ 760.00	×	24	= $	_____
25.	$1,062.84	×	24	= $	_____
26.	$1,141.00	×	24	= $	_____
27.	$ 840.90	×	24	= $	_____
28.	$ 816.66	×	24	= $	_____
29.	$ 925.00	×	24	= $	_____
30.	$ 465.00	×	52	= $	_____
31.	$ 538.75	×	52	= $	_____
32.	$ 512.00	×	52	= $	_____
33.	$ 399.25	×	52	= $	_____
34.	$ 325.00	×	52	= $	_____
35.	$ 408.75	×	52	= $	_____

CONSTANT DIVISION

In constant division, the divisor (the second number in the problem) is the constant factor. The divisor is always the second number entered.

Demonstration Problem

Estimate $17,220 ÷ 52 as 20,000 ÷ 50 = 400.

Annual Salary		Constant Divisor		Weekly Salary
$17,220	÷	52	=	$331.15
$22,140	÷	52	=	$425.77
$25,630	÷	52	=	$492.88
$28,400	÷	52	=	$546.15
$33,390	÷	52	=	$642.12

Compared to the estimate, $331.15 is reasonable.

1. Set for a two-decimal-place answer.

2. Set the Round switch in the five/four position.

3. Set the calculator in the Constant Operation mode. (See the instruction manual for your calculator.)

Enter	Press	Tape	Screen
	T	0.00 T	0.
17,220	÷	17,220.00 ÷	17,220.
52	=	52.00 =	52.
		331.15	331.15
22,140	=	22,140.00 =	22,140.
		425.77	425.77
25,630	=	25,630.00 =	25,630.
		492.88	492.88
28,400	=	28,400.00 =	28,400.
		546.15	546.15
33,390	=	33,390.00 =	33,390.
		642.12	642.12

Use the constant divisor 52 to find the weekly salaries of the annual salaries listed in Problems 36 through 43. Check Problem C before you work Problems 36 through 43.

Round money amounts to two decimal places. Record your answers for Problems 36 through 50 on the Answer Tab for Lesson 8.

Use the constant divisor 24 to find the semimonthly salaries of the annual salaries listed in Problems 44 through 50. Semimonthly salaries are paid twice each month. Check Problem D before completing the rest of the problems.

	Annual Salary	Weekly Salary (Use a Divisor of 52)
C.	$16,900	$ 325.00
36.	$18,250	$
37.	$19,050	$
38.	$20,354	$
39.	$21,097	$
40.	$23,098	$
41.	$25,372	$
42.	$27,075	$
43.	$29,257	$

	Annual Salary	Semimonthly Salary (Use a Divisor of 24)
D.	$17,389	$ 724.54
44.	$18,536	$
45.	$19,574	$
46.	$21,190	$
47.	$22,063	$
48.	$23,208	$
49.	$26,942	$
50.	$27,900	$

Many small items are sold by the gross. There are 144 items in 1 gross. In Problems 51 through 57, find the number of gross in each set of items. Your constant divisor will be 144. Round your answers to three decimal places. Check Problem E, estimate your answers, and then proceed to Problems 51 through 57.

The first column in Problems 58 through 64 gives the price per gross. Find the unit price by dividing the gross price by 144, which will be your constant divisor. Round your answers to the nearest cent. Check Problem F.

Remember to record your answers on the Answer Tab for Lesson 8.

	Number of Items		Constant Divisor		Number of Gross
E.	768	÷	144	=	5,333
51.	900	÷	144	=	
52.	1,116	÷	144	=	
53.	1,200	÷	144	=	
54.	528	÷	144	=	
55.	1,512	÷	144	=	
56.	888	÷	144	=	
57.	635	÷	144	=	

	Price per Gross		Constant Divisor		Price per Item
F.	$ 100	÷	144	=	$ .69
58.	$ 111.90	÷	144	=	$
59.	$ 845.10	÷	144	=	$
60.	$1,000.00	÷	144	=	$
61.	$ 248.00	÷	144	=	$
62.	$ 72.00	÷	144	=	$
63.	$ 615.75	÷	144	=	$
64.	$ 409.00	÷	144	=	$

Business Application

PRICE PER OUNCE. Many supermarkets show the price per ounce on their shelf price tags. Customers can thus compare the prices of different sizes of the same item.

Which of the following bottles of mouthwash has the lowest price per ounce?

Price	Weight in Oz.	Price per Oz.	Lowest Price per Oz.
$1.99 ÷	9	= $.2211	
$2.87 ÷	16	= $.1794	
$3.19 ÷	24	− $.1329	✓

In Problems 65 through 69, estimate first. Then divide the price by the number of ounces to find the price per ounce. Round your answer to four decimal places. Check (✓) the lowest price per ounce for each item. Record your answers for Problems 65 through 70 on the Answer Tab for Lesson 8.

Item	Price	Weight in Oz.	Price per Oz.	Lowest Price per Oz.
65. Orange juice	$ 1.09	8	$ _____	_____
	$ 1.69	16	$ _____	_____
	$ 2.29	32	$ _____	_____
66. Toothpaste	$ .79	2	$ _____	_____
	$ 1.69	5	$ _____	_____
	$ 2.19	9	$ _____	_____
67. White beans	$ .63	8	$ _____	_____
	$ .98	16	$ _____	_____
	$ 1.79	32	$ _____	_____
68. Butter	$ 1.19	8	$ _____	_____
	$ 1.98	16	$ _____	_____
69. Salad oil	$ 1.89	16	$ _____	_____
	$ 3.29	32	$ _____	_____
	$ 3.98	48	$ _____	_____

70. Communication Define *constant factor.*

MULTIPLYING THREE OR MORE FACTORS

CONTINUOUS MULTIPLICATION

Set for a two-decimal-place answer.

Estimate: $40 \times 70 \times 1 = 2,800$

THREE-FACTOR MULTIPLICATION

The multiplication of three factors in one problem can be done in two ways. One way is called *continuous multiplication*.

Remember to estimate your answers.

Demonstration Problem

First Factor		Second Factor		Third Factor		Product
38	×	72	×	.98	=	2,681.28

Continuous multiplication, sometimes called *chain multiplication*, is shown at the right.

Enter	Press	Tape	Screen
	T	0.00 T	0.
38	×	38.00 ×	38.
72	×	72.00 ×	72.
			2,736.
.98	=	0.98 =	0.98
		2,681.28	2,681.28

Compared to the estimate, the answer is reasonable.

The second method of three-factor multiplication is called *noncontinuous multiplication*. It is demonstrated at the right.

First, find the product of two factors. Then multiply that product by the third factor.

Be sure to check the instructions for your calculator.

After you have worked the demonstration problem, check the answers to Problems A and B. Set your calculator for a two-decimal-place answer.

Estimates:

A. $10 \times 30 \times 60 = 18,000$
B. $80 \times 80 \times \frac{1}{4} = 1,600$

Compared to the estimates, the answers are reasonable.

NONCONTINUOUS MULTIPLICATION

Set your calculator for a two-decimal-place answer.

Enter	Press	Tape	Screen
	T	0.00 T	0.
38	×	38.00 ×	38.
72	=	72.00 =	72.
		2,736.00	2,736.
	×	2,736.00 ×	2,736
.98	=	0.98 =	0.98
		2,681.28	2,681.28

	First Factor		Second Factor		Third Factor		Product
A.	12	×	34	×	56	=	22,848.
B.	79	×	81	×	.25	=	1,599.75

Estimate first. Then record your answers for Problems 1 through 51 on the Answer Tab for Lesson 9.

Set your Decimal Point Selector for as many places as are required in the multiplication problem, unless directed to do otherwise. Remember that in multiplication you must add the decimal places in each multiplier, which will give you the required number of decimal places.

Demonstration Problem

Estimate: $1.6 \times 31.2 \times 9.47$ as
$2 \times 30 \times 9 = 540$.

$1.6 \times 31.2 \times 9.47 = 472.7424$

Compared to the estimate, the answer is reasonable.

The decimal places in the problem total four $(1 + 1 + 2 \text{ places})$. Note the four decimal places in the answer.

1. 21	×	63	×	69	= _____
2. 1.8	×	3.43	×	36	= _____
3. 23	×	50	×	.96	= _____
4. 94	×	5.03	×	7.8	= _____
5. 54	×	91	×	.05	= _____
6. 428	×	54	×	.75	= _____
7. 165	×	48	×	.33	= _____
8. 85	×	5	×	6.75	= _____
9. 8.5	×	36	×	3.6	= _____
10. 567	×	2.19	×	72	= _____
11. 325	×	.75	×	1.25	= _____
12. 547	×	1.75	×	.25	= _____

Business Application 1

Office space is usually rented by the square foot. Three factors are used in finding the cost of office rental space. They are (1) length, (2) width, and (3) cost per square foot. Multiply the length in feet times the width in feet to find the area in square feet. Multiply the area times the cost per square foot to find the rental charge.

Because the multiplication involves dollars and cents, the Decimal Point Selector should be set at two.

Demonstration Problem

Estimate: 24 × 12 × $14.70 as 30 × 10 × 15
= 4,500.

Length in Ft.	Width in Ft.	Cost per Sq. Ft.	Rental Charge
24 ×	12 ×	$14.70 =	$4,233.60

Compared to the estimate, $4,233.60 is reasonable.

Estimate first. Then record your answers on the answer tab for Lesson 9.

	Length in Ft.		Width in Ft.		Cost per Sq. Ft.		Rental Charge
13.	12	×	12	×	$ 9.50	= $	_____
14.	17.5	×	14	×	$ 8.75	= $	_____
15.	24.5	×	18	×	$ 9.25	= $	_____
16.	40	×	45	×	$ 9.75	= $	_____
17.	50	×	50	×	$10.75	= $	_____
18.	110	×	75	×	$11.25	= $	_____
19.	75	×	125	×	$12.00	= $	_____
20.	35.5	×	47.5	×	$11.55	= $	_____
21.	44.5	×	32.75	×	$10.25	= $	_____
22.	85	×	45.5	×	$12.25	= $	_____
23.	100	×	68.5	×	$11.75	= $	_____
24.	85	×	48.5	×	$ 9.90	= $	_____

Business Application 2

Sales taxes are added to the selling price of many items in most states and in some cities. To find the total amount of the sale, multiply the quantity sold times the price per item times the sales tax factor.

In Problems 25 through 36, the sales tax has been added to 100% to give a factor for finding the total sale in a continuous multiplication operation. The factor 1.02 is used to add a city sales tax of 2%, 1.05 is used to add a state sales tax of 5%, and 1.07 is used to add a combined city and state sales tax of 7%.

Remember to estimate your answers first.

Demonstration Problem

Estimate $6 \times 12.95 \times 1.02$ as $10 \times 10 \times 1 = 100$.

Qty. Sold	Price per Item	Sales Tax Factor	Total Sale
6	× $12.95	× 1.02	= $79.25

Compared to the estimate, $79.25 is reasonable.

	Qty. Sold		Price per Item		Sales Tax Factor		Total Sale
25.	4	×	$ 9.95	×	1.02	=	$_____
26.	15	×	$ 2.97	×	1.02	=	$_____
27.	6	×	$10.75	×	1.02	=	$_____
28.	5	×	$24.99	×	1.02	=	$_____
29.	17	×	$ 2.79	×	1.05	=	$_____
30.	22	×	$ 1.69	×	1.05	=	$_____
31.	8	×	$ 3.89	×	1.05	=	$_____
32.	39	×	$ 1.39	×	1.05	=	$_____
33.	2	×	$65.97	×	1.07	=	$_____
34.	5	×	$99.98	×	1.07	=	$_____
35.	4	×	$26.75	×	1.07	=	$_____
36.	3	×	$69.98	×	1.07	=	$_____

MULTIPLYING WITH MORE THAN THREE FACTORS

The methods used for multiplying with three factors are also used for multiplying with more than three factors.

Solve Problems 37 through 50. Estimate first. Set the decimal selector at five and round your answers manually to four decimal places.

Demonstration Problem

Estimate $75 \times 6.5 \times .13 \times 1.45$ as
$$80 \times 10 \times .1 \times 1 = 80.$$

$75 \times 6.5 \times .13 \times 1.45 \qquad = 91.89375$
Rounded to four places = 91.8938

Compared to the estimate, the answer is reasonable.

Record your answers for Problems 37 through 51 on the Answer Tab for Lesson 9.

After you complete Lesson 9, check with your instructor about taking Progress Test 5 on pages 226 and 227.

37.	.39	×	1.25	×	13	×	6.6	= _____
38.	1.444	×	12	×	10	×	2.29	= _____
39.	360	×	11	×	.6275	×	3.64	= _____
40.	12	×	13	×	15	×	.4444	= _____
41.	56.34	×	8	×	9	×	12.643	= _____
42.	.36	×	39.5	×	78.8	×	9.91	= _____
43.	22.56	×	1.58	×	47	×	12.34	= _____
44.	.6	×	.12	×	979	×	1.111	= _____
45.	4	×	8	×	16	×	.6464	= _____
46.	8	×	16	×	48	×	.53232	= _____
47.	10	×	20	×	.15	×	3.3333	= _____
48.	27	×	3	×	.81	×	9.123	= _____
49.	12.5	×	4.4	×	2.5	×	.682	= _____
50.	5.45	×	6.36	×	7.27	×	8.18	= _____

51. Communication   Explain continuous multiplication.

LESSON 10

MIXED OPERATIONS

ADDITION AND SUBTRACTION FOLLOWED BY MULTIPLICATION OR DIVISION

A number of business problems use some combination of addition, subtraction, multiplication, and division, which is called a **mixed operation**.

Demonstration Problems

$$(25 + 18 - 19) \times 4 = 96$$
$$24 \qquad \times 4 = 96$$
$$(25 + 18 - 19) \div 4 = 6$$
$$24 \qquad \div 4 = 6$$

(Do the operations in parentheses first.)

Mixed operations can be done in a continuous process on most calculators. After addition or subtraction, press the Total key. Pressing the Multiplication or Division key will automatically print that total again. Then enter the factor or divisor. (NOTE: From now on only the tape printout will be shown. It clearly shows the sequence of operations.) See the instructions for your calculator for mixed operations.

$$(25 + 18 - 19) \times 4 = 96$$

Estimate: $(30 + 20 - 20) \times 4 = 120$

Enter	Press	Tape
	T	0. T
25	+	25. +
18	+	18. +
19	−	19. −
	T	24. T
	×	24. ×
4	=	4. =
		96.

$$(25 + 18 - 19) \div 4 = 6$$

Estimate: $(30 + 20 - 20) \div 4 \approx 4$

Enter	Press	Tape
	T	0. T
25	+	25. +
18	+	18. +
19	−	19. −
	T	24. T
	÷	24. ÷
4	=	4. =
		6.

Compared to the estimates, the answers are reasonable.

Set the Decimal Point Selector at zero to work the demonstration problems and to check Problems A and B. Estimate the answers to Problems 1 through 18 first. Then solve Problems 1 through 10.

Set the Decimal Point Selector at three for Problems C, D, and 11 through 18. Round your answers to two decimal places.

Record your answers for Problems 1 through 18 on the Answer Tab for Lesson 10.

A. $(8 + 9 - 3)$ $\times$ 6 = <u>84</u>

B. $(10 + 11 - 4)$ $\times$ 11 = <u>187</u>

1. $(124 + 136 - 70)$ $\times$ 10 = _____

2. $(23 + 71 - 40)$ $\times$ 8 = _____

3. $(89 - 38 + 8)$ $\times$ 11 = _____

4. $(156 - 132 + 24)$ $\times$ 14 = _____

5. $(29 + 15 - 3)$ $\times$ 6 = _____

6. $(143 - 13 + 127)$ $\times$ 4 = _____

7. $(17 + 18 - 4)$ $\times$ 13 = _____

8. $(415 - 236 + 100)$ $\times$ 8 = _____

9. $(121 - 13 - 12)$ $\times$ 15 = _____

10. $(239 - 15 + 87)$ $\times$ 19 = _____

C. $(28 - 15 + 12)$ $\div$ 4 = <u>6.25</u>

D. $(186 - 37 + 202)$ $\div$ 17 = <u>20.65</u>

11. $(295 - 143 + 350)$ $\div$ 32 = _____

12. $(2,985 - 1,084)$ $\div$ 72 = _____

13. $(5,899 - 1,202)$ $\div$ 180 = _____

14. $(543 + 678)$ $\div$ 24 = _____

15. $(8,435 - 3,282)$ $\div$ 730 = _____

16. $(2,079 - 345)$ $\div$ 58 = _____

17. $(765 + 342 - 89)$ $\div$ 74 = _____

18. $(5,421 - 1,369)$ $\div$ 720 — _____

Business Application 1

A sales summary report is used to show weekly and total sales by department. Averages are used by businesses to learn about trends of past sales and to forecast future sales.

Estimate. Then, find the total sales for each department and divide by 4 to find the average weekly sales. Do crossfooting and total the sales for each week. The total weekly sales should agree with the total departmental sales. Divide the total sales by 4 to find the average weekly sales (Answer 30).

Check Problems E and F. Record your answers for Problems 19 through 30 on the Answer Tab for Lesson 10.

FOUR-WEEK SALES SUMMARY

Department	Week 1	Week 2	Week 3	Week 4	Total Sales		Average Weekly Sales	
Small appliances	$21,200	$19,700	$25,800	$26,700	$93,400	E.	$23,350	F.
Electronics	18,600	18,500	19,300	29,400	$_____	19.	$_____	20.
Linens	19,300	22,300	24,400	28,200	$_____	21.	$_____	22.
Garden shop	17,200	16,800	19,300	20,100	$_____	23.	$_____	24.
TOTALS	$_____	$_____	$_____	$_____	$_____		$_____	
	25.	26.	27.	28.	29.			30.

MULTIPLICATION OR DIVISION FOLLOWED BY ADDITION OR SUBTRACTION

Do all operations in parentheses first. Press the Equals key to get the multiplication or division answer. Then press the Plus key to enter that answer for addition or subtraction.

Demonstration Problems

$(15 \times 12) - 25 = 155$
$180 \qquad - 25 = 155$

$(156 \div 13) + 25 = 37$
$12 \qquad + 25 = 37$

Work the demonstration problems with Decimal Point Selector at zero. Then, set the Decimal Point Selector at three. Check Problems G and H. Estimate. Round your answers for Problems 31 through 40 to two decimal places. Record your answers for Problems 31 through 40 on the Answer Tab for Lesson 10.

$(15 \times 12) - 25 = 155$

Estimate: $(20 \times 10) - 30 = 170$

Enter	Press	Tape
	T	0. T
15	×	15. ×
12	=	12. =
		180.
	+	180. +
25	−	25. −
	T	155. T

$(156 \div 13) + 25 = 37$

Estimate: $(200 \div 10) + 30 = 50$

Enter	Press	Tape
	T	0. T
156	÷	156. ÷
13	=	13. =
		12.
	+	12. +
25	+	25. +
	T	37. T

Compared to the estimates, the answers are reasonable.

G. $(4.5 \times 6.3) + 22.4 = $ _50.75_

H. $(1,386 \div 24) - 16 = $ _41.75_

31. $(19 \times 5) - 19 = $ _____

32. $(232 \times 15) - 48 = $ _____

33. $(5 \times 5) + 25 = $ _____

34. $(151 \times 11) + 2,513 = $ _____

35. $(5.25 \times 8.4) + 18.4 = $ _____

36. $(1,809 \div 76) + 62 = $ _____

37. $(26.88 \div 2.6) + 15.2 = $ _____

38. $(15,288 \div 58.11) + 22.5 = $ _____

39. $(3,001.54 \div 16.25) - 88.6 = $ _____

40. $(4,151.5 \div 12.75) - 98.7 = $ _____

MIXED OPERATIONS OF MULTIPLICATION AND DIVISION

Mixed calculations of multiplication and division are done in a continuous operation. If a noncontinuous operation is required by your calculator, complete the first operation by pressing the Equals key. Then the next operation is continued. Check the manual for your calculator.

Demonstration Problems

$$(12 \times 8) \div 16 = 6$$
$$96 \qquad \div 16 = 6$$

$$(168 \div 12) \times 6 = 84$$
$$14 \qquad \times 6 = 84$$

Work the demonstration problems with Decimal Point Selector at zero. Then, set the Decimal Point Selector at three. Check Problems I and J. Estimate. Round your answers for Problems 41 through 50 to two decimal places. Record your answers for Problems 41 through 50 on the Answer Tab for Lesson 10.

Continuous operation of multiplication and division requires three steps: $\boxed{\times}$, $\boxed{\div}$, and $\boxed{=}$ or $\boxed{\div}$, $\boxed{\times}$, and $\boxed{=}$.

$$(12 \times 8) \div 16 = 6$$

Enter	Press	Tape
	T	0. T
12	×	12. ×
8	÷	8. ÷
16	=	16. =
		6.

$$(168 \div 12) \times 6 = 84$$

Enter	Press	Tape
	T	0. T
168	÷	168. ÷
12	×	12. ×
6	=	6. =
		84.

I. $(14 \times 7) \div 6 \qquad = \underline{\ 16.33\ }$

J. $(96 \div 16) \times 11 \qquad = \underline{\ 66\ }$

41. $(108 \times 45) \div 72 \qquad = \underline{\qquad}$

42. $(3,960 \times 67.5) \div 180 = \underline{\qquad}$

43. $(68.5 \times 29.4) \div 109 \quad = \underline{\qquad}$

44. $(25.2 \times 38) \div 12.5 \quad = \underline{\qquad}$

45. $(12.5 \times 12.5) \div 2.1 \qquad = \underline{\qquad}$

46. $(7,952 \div 32) \times 24.5 \qquad = \underline{\qquad}$

47. $(45.92 \div 8.2) \times 9.75 \qquad = \underline{\qquad}$

48. $(10.8 \div 1.8) \times 11.375 \quad = \underline{\qquad}$

49. $(120.69 \div 14.9) \times 3.875 = \underline{\qquad}$

50. $(789 \div 12) \times 52.5 \qquad = \underline{\qquad}$

Business Application 2

A payroll register is a record prepared at the end of each pay period. It shows the hours worked, hourly rate of pay, gross earnings, deductions, and net pay for each employee. The employees' checks and accounting entries are prepared from this record.

Total Hours Worked × Rate per Hour = Gross Pay

Gross Pay − Deductions = Net Pay

Complete the payroll register. Check Problems K and L. Estimate. Then set your Decimal Point Selector at two for money amounts. Work Problems 51 through 66 and record your answers for Problems 51 through 67 on the Answer Tab for Lesson 10.

PAYROLL REGISTER: WEEK OF JANUARY 2–6

Employee	Total Hours Worked	Rate per Hour	Gross Pay		Deductions	Net Pay	
A. Arnold	39.75	$5.75	$228.56	K.	$19.00	$209.56	L.
D. Chung	39	6.55	_____	51.	18.53	_____	52.
U. David	37.5	6.40	_____	53.	19.75	_____	54.
F. Falk	38.25	6.85	_____	55.	21.38	_____	56.
P. Goya	35.5	7.25	_____	57.	17.98	_____	58.
H. Helman	36.75	7.00	_____	59.	22.64	_____	60.
I. Nguyen	40	7.50	_____	61.	29.50	_____	62.
S. Samuels	39.5	7.25	_____	63.	24.10	_____	64.
X. Thomas	38.5	6.95	_____	65.	21.98	_____	66.

67. Communication   What are mixed operations?

ACCUMULATIVE MULTIPLICATION

ACCUMULATIVE MULTIPLICATION

OBJECTIVE

- *Add multiplication products using the memory function.*

ACCUMULATIVE MULTIPLICATION

The addition of multiplication products is called **accumulative multiplication**. Accumulative multiplication is performed as a continuous process on all electronic calculators equipped with at least one Memory Register.

If your calculator does not have a Memory Register, you must add the products of each multiplication problem in a separate operation.

Calculators that can perform the accumulative multiplication process have special keys:

$=+$ and $=-$, $M+$ and $M-$, $I+$ and $I-$, or $M\pm$ and $M\equiv$.

These keys are in addition to the regular $+$ and $-$ keys.

The principle of accumulative multiplication is the same on all calculators with a Memory Register. You do the separate multiplications in the usual manner, but use one of the Memory keys to accumulate each product in the Memory Register. To recall what is in memory, press the MR , RM , $M\Diamond$, or other memory recall key on your calculator. The sum of the products is printed on the tape or displayed on the screen.

Read the instructions for your calculator to learn how to use its accumulative multiplication mode.

Demonstration Problem

5 watches at	$29.95 =	$149.75
3 clock radios at	49.95 =	149.85
7 lamps at	59.95 =	419.65
	TOTAL =	$719.25

Below are examples of two calculator tapes for the above problem:

0.00	T	0.00	T
5.00	×	5.00	×
29.95	=	29.95	= +
149.75	ᵐ₊	149.75	*
3.00	×	3.00	×
49.95	=	49.95	= +
149.85	ᵐ₊	149.85	*
7.00	×	7.00	×
59.95	=	59.95	= +
419.65	ᵐ₊	419.65	*
719.25	ᵐ*	719.25	*

The steps given below for solving the demonstration problem are general because the specific method of entering the products into the Memory Register varies from calculator to calculator. Read the instructions for accumulative multiplication for your calculator.

1. Set the Decimal Point Selector at two and the Round switch in the five/four position.

2. Clear the calculator and the Memory Register.

3. Remember to estimate your answers first.

4. Multiply 5 times 29.95.

5. Enter the product (149.75) into the Memory Register.

6. Multiply 3 times 49.95.

7. Enter the product (149.85) into the Memory Register.

8. Multiply 7 times 59.95.

9. Enter the product (419.65) into the Memory Register.

10. Take the total by recalling the products from the Memory Register: 719.25.

Check the estimates and answers given for Problems A and B. Always estimate before solving the problem. If your estimated answer is close to your calculated answer, your solution is probably correct.

A. Set the Decimal Point Selector at zero.

287	×	24	=	6,888
192	×	49	=	9,408
305	×	79	=	24,095
				40,391

Estimate

300	×	20	=	6,000
200	×	50	=	10,000
300	×	80	=	24,000
				40,000

B.

Quantity	Description	Unit Price	Extension
6 pr.	Driving gloves	$ 8.98	$ 53.88
4	Shoulder bags	17.99	71.96
8 pr.	Pigskin gloves	10.49	83.92
		TOTAL	$209.76

Estimate

6	×	$10	=	$ 60.00
4	×	20	=	80.00
8	×	10	=	80.00
		TOTAL	=	$220.00

Set the Decimal Point Selector at zero for accumulative multiplication in Problems 1 through 10. Estimate the answers for the problems as indicated. Write your estimated answers and your calculator answers on the Answer Tab for Lesson 11.

1.

8 × 9 = _____

5 × 7 = _____

_____ T

2.

9 × 9 = _____

7 × 7 = _____

_____ T

3.

	Estimate
28 × 11	= 30 × 10 = 300
21 × 12	= _____
24 × 16	= _____
	_____ T

4. Calculator Answer

308
_____
_____
_____ T

5.

	Estimate
144 × 8	= _____
55 × 19	= _____
95 × 13	= _____
	_____ T

6. Calculator Answer

_____
_____
_____
_____ T

7.

	Estimate
175 × 12	= _____
36 × 12	= _____
95 × 52	= _____
108 × 52	= _____
	_____ T

8. Calculator Answer

_____
_____
_____
_____ T

9.

	Estimate
197 × 31	= _____
4,250 × 11	= _____
596 × 102	= _____
2,958 × 12	= _____
	_____ T

10. Calculator Answer

_____
_____
_____
_____ T

Estimate first. Set the Decimal Point Selector at three and mentally round your totals to two decimal places in Problems 11 through 18. Check Problems C and D first.

$$35.67 \times 1.22 = \underline{43.517}$$
$$325. \times .123 = \underline{39.975}$$
$$15.23 \times 9.87 = \underline{150.320}$$
$$\underline{233.812} \text{ T } \textbf{C.}$$

Rounded to two
decimal places   233.81 T **D.**

Record your answers on the Answer Tab for Lesson 11.

$$17.5 \times 8.57 = \underline{\hspace{2cm}}$$
$$8.33 \times 15.45 = \underline{\hspace{2cm}}$$

$$\underline{\hspace{2cm}} \text{ T } \textbf{11.}$$

Rounded to two
decimal places $\underline{\hspace{2cm}}$ T **12.**

$$5.375 \times 313. = \underline{\hspace{2cm}}$$
$$.333 \times 97. = \underline{\hspace{2cm}}$$

$$\underline{\hspace{2cm}} \text{ T } \textbf{15.}$$

Rounded to two
decimal places $\underline{\hspace{2cm}}$ T **16.**

$$14.52 \times 133.57 = \underline{\hspace{2cm}}$$
$$50.75 \times 6.74 = \underline{\hspace{2cm}}$$

$$\underline{\hspace{2cm}} \text{ T } \textbf{13.}$$

Rounded to two
decimal places $\underline{\hspace{2cm}}$ T **14.**

$$442.3 \times 4.33 = \underline{\hspace{2cm}}$$
$$111.5 \times 53.75 = \underline{\hspace{2cm}}$$
$$2.19 \times .75 = \underline{\hspace{2cm}}$$

$$\underline{\hspace{2cm}} \text{ T } \textbf{17.}$$

Rounded to two
decimal places $\underline{\hspace{2cm}}$ T **18.**

Business Application 1

CHECKING INVOICES. Use accumulative multiplication to check the accuracy of the invoice items in Problems 19 through 30. Put a check mark after each correct amount. Record the correct amount where you find an error.

Two common errors are shown in the problems: (1) pressing the wrong number key and (2) transposing numbers when copying the numbers that appear on the tape. For example, *transposing* means writing 35 for 53.

Estimate first. Check Problems E and F before solving the remaining problems. The check problems are part of the total. Set the Decimal Point Selector at two. Record your answers on the Answer Tab for Lesson 11.

POE'S POTTERY BARN
1250 Main Street
Paris, TX 75460

Invoice No. 5801

Date 10/18/- -

Terms Cash

Sold to J. Gomez
5 Elm Street
Paris, TX 75460

Quantity	Description	Unit Price	Extension	Checking	
16	Dinner plates	$10.77	$127.32	$172.32	E.
16	Salad bowls	$10.05	$160.80	✓	F.
16	Dessert plates	$ 8.37	$133.92		19.
16	Saucers	$ 6.75	$ 94.50		20.
16	Cups	$ 6.87	$109.29		21.
4	Vegetable dishes	$21.75	$ 87.00		22.
2	Gravy boats	$17.97	$ 39.54		23.
4	Butter dishes	$22.05	$ 82.80		24.
2	Sugar bowls	$ 8.67	$ 17.34		25.
4	Large platters	$32.94	$113.76		26.
4	Small platters	$20.64	$ 82.65		27.
2	Creamers	$ 9.45	$ 18.90		28.
6	Medium platters	$26.25	$175.50		29.
	TOTAL		$1,243.32		30.

Business Application 2

EXTENDING PURCHASE ORDERS.

Estimate first. Use accumulative multiplication to find the extensions and totals for the purchase orders in Problems 31 through 38. Multiply the quantity by the unit price to find the extension. Accumulate the extensions to find the total.

Remember that the Decimal Point Selector for money amounts is two decimal places. Record your answers for Problems 31 through 39 on the Answer Tab for Lesson 11.

ARROW DISTRIBUTORS
2411 Balboa Avenue
San Francisco, California 94120

Sporting Goods Unlimited
12 Van Ness
San Francisco, CA 94123

PURCHASE ORDER

Date Issued 10/11/--	Date Needed 11/20/--	Requisition No. 1001	Terms Cash
Via UPS		FOB - -	

Quantity	Description	Unit Price	Extension
9	6-qt coolers	$13.50	$ _____
8	4-gal coolers	$21.00	$ _____
7	Charcoal grills	$25.50	$ _____
6	Sleeping bags	$37.50	$ _____
		TOTAL	$ _____

31.

Quantity	Description	Unit Price	Extension
16	Tennis rackets	$30.49	$ _____
15	Basketballs	$24.89	$ _____
14	Roller skates	$27.99	$ _____
13	Baseball gloves	$30.29	$ _____
		TOTAL	$ _____

32.

Remember to record your answers on the Answer Tab for Lesson 11.

Quantity	Description	Unit Price	Extension
8	Ski jackets	$55.00	$ _____
8	Ski sweaters	$34.90	$ _____
24	Sport shirts	$19.50	$ _____
12	Rib sweaters	$38.50	$
		TOTAL	$ _____

33.

Quantity	Description	Unit Price	Extension
4	Cashmere pullovers	$59.50	$ _____
5	Tennis sweaters	$37.00	$ _____
6	Crew neck sweaters	$25.96	$ _____
7	Sport shirts	$24.50	$ _____
		TOTAL	$ _____

34.

Remember to record your answers on the Answer Tab for Lesson 11.

Quantity	Description	Unit Price	Extension
4	Calendar watches	$59.50	$ _____
8	Sport watches	$53.96	$ _____
12	Key rings	$21.00	$ _____
10	Cuff links	$31.98	$ _____
		TOTAL	$ _____

35.

Quantity	Description	Unit Price	Extension
6	Golf jackets	$67.50	$ _____
12	Knit shirts	$26.94	$ _____
12	Turtleneck shirts	$47.94	$ _____
6	Sleeveless pullovers	$31.50	$ _____
		TOTAL	$ _____

36.

Remember to record your answers on the Answer Tab for Lesson 11.

Quantity	Description	Unit Price	Extension
9	Assorted chocolates	$ 9.96	$ _____
11	California candy	$10.50	$ _____
6	Fruitcakes	$ 9.18	$ _____
7	Nut assortments	$10.98	$ _____
		TOTAL	$ _____

37.

38. Communication   Explain accumulative multiplication.

39. Communication   Give an example of transposing numbers.

NEGATIVE MULTIPLICATION

NEGATIVE MULTIPLICATION

Negative multiplication takes place when one multiplication product is subtracted from another multiplication product.

Demonstration Problem

$$(15 \times 11) - (8 \times 8) = 101$$
$$165 - 64 = 101$$

Negative multiplication can be done in a continuous process on all electronic calculators equipped with a Memory Register.

1. Estimate $(15 \times 11) - (8 \times 8) = 101$ as
   $(20 \times 10) - (10 \times 10) = 100$.

2. Clear the calculator and the Memory Register.   0. T

3. Set the Decimal Point Selector at zero.   15. ×

4. Multiply 15 by 11.   11. = +

5. Enter the product (165) into the Memory Register.   165. *

6. Multiply 8 by 8.   8. ×

7. Enter the product into the Memory Register as a negative number (−64). Use the ⌷=−⌷, ⌷M−⌷, ⌷I−⌷, or ⌷M≡⌷ key.   8. = −   64. *

8. Recall the remainder from the Memory Register. Use the ⌷T⌷, ⌷MR⌷, ⌷*⌷, or ⌷RM⌷ key. (See the instructions for your calculator.)   101. *

For calculators with a Memory Register, the procedure for negative multiplication is the same as for accumulative multiplication with one exception. One product is subtracted from the Memory Register with one of the following keys: =−, M−, I−, or M≡.

For calculators without a Memory Register, the two multiplication problems must be calculated separately. The subtraction of one product from the other must be done in a separate operation.

Work the demonstration problem and check Problems A and B.

These are the steps for negative multiplication on a calculator without a Memory Register. A sample tape is shown at the right.

	Tape
1. Clear the calculator.	0. T
2. Multiply 15 by 11.	15. ×
3. Write down your answer (165) if your calculator has a display.	11. =
4. Multiply 8 by 8.	165. *
	8. ×
	8. =
5. Write down your answer (64).	64. *
	165. +
	64. −
6. Subtract: 165 − 64 = 101.	101. *

	Positive Multiplication		Negative Multiplication		Remainder
A.	(13×12)	−	(11×9)	=	57
B.	(365×102)	−	(256×125)	=	5,230

Estimate. Then solve Problems 1 through 15. Set your calculator for a two-decimal-place answer.

Record your answers on the Answer Tab for Lesson 12.

1. $(14 \times 15) - (11 \times 12) = $ _____

2. $(67 \times 23) - (41 \times 35) = $ _____

3. $(92 \times 46) - (74 \times 30) = $ _____

4. $(125 \times 10.8) - (110 \times .99) = $ _____

5. $(190 \times 73) - (18.2 \times 72) = $ _____

6. $(475 \times 232) - (240 \times 24.2) = $ _____

7. $(9.25 \times 6.5) - (7.75 \times 4.1) = $ _____

8. $(9.67 \times 5.33) - (8.25 \times 4.1) = $ _____

9. $(88.8 \times 9.05) - (76.6 \times 6.05) = $ _____

10. $(55.5 \times 24.3) - (28 \times 25) = $ _____

11. $(36 \times 2.98) - (6 \times 1.47) = $ _____

12. $(258 \times 1.45) - (13 \times 1.67) = $ _____

13. $(78 \times 12.99) - (3 \times 13.99) = $ _____

14. $(193 \times 2.5) - (29 \times 1.45) = $ _____

15. $(78 \times 13.5) - (12 \times 12.67) = $ _____

Business Application

Estimate and complete the sales slips in Problems 16 through 24. Use negative multiplication to find the amount of the sale, the amount of the return (to be deducted), and the difference still due.

Work the demonstration problem below before proceeding with Problems 16 through 25.

Demonstration Problem

$$
\begin{array}{rl}
15 \text{ items @ } \$5.97 & = \quad \$\ 89.55 \\
\text{Returned 4 items @ } 3.79 & = \quad -15.16 \\
\text{Difference} & \quad \$\ 74.39
\end{array}
$$

(The expression @ **$5.97** means at $5.97 per item.)

Record your answers to Problems 16 through 25 on the Answer Tab for Lesson 12.

Quantity	Description	Unit Price	Extension	
4 gal.	Latex paint	$10.98	$ _____	**16.**
2 gal.	Paint returned	8.98	− $ _____	**17.**
		Difference	$ _____	**18.**

Quantity	Description	Unit Price	Extension	
6	Spray enamel	$ 2.98	$ _____	**19.**
3	Enamel returned	1.29	− $ _____	**20.**
		Difference	$ _____	**21.**

Quantity	Description	Unit Price	Extension	
24	$3\frac{1}{2}''$ Masking tape	$ 2.88	$ _____	**22.**
12	2″ Masking tape returned	1.99	− $ _____	**23.**
		Difference	$ _____	**24.**

25. Communication What is *negative multiplication*?

Solving some of the problems on the TI BA-35 Solar calculator requires different instructions than those given in the lessons.

There is no constant key or automatic constant register on the TI BA-35 Solar calculator, so the first factor entered will not be a constant.

Using Memory Keys for Repeated Operations

The demonstration problem from page 46 is shown at the right. The steps for *constant multiplication* on a TI BA-35 Solar calculator are as follows.

Hourly Rate		Hours Worked		Total Pay
$3.96	×	8	=	$ 31.68
$3.96	×	16	=	$ 63.36
$3.96	×	32	=	$126.72
$3.96	×	37.5	=	$148.50

1. Enter 3 [.] 96 and press STO to store 3.96 in memory.

2. Multiply by 8 to get the product 31.68.

3. Recall 3.96 by pressing RCL 2nd [MEM].

4. Multiply by 16 to get 63.36.

> 3 [.] 96 STO [×] 8 [=] 31.68 RCL 2nd [MEM] [×] 16 [=] 63.36

Continue recalling 3.96 and multiply by 32 to get 126.72. Recall 3.96 and multiply by 37.5 to get the product 148.50.

> RCL 2nd [MEM] [×] 32 [=] 126.72 RCL 2nd [MEM] [×] 37 [.] 5 [=] 148.50

Solve. Write your answers on a separate sheet of paper.

1. $2.34 × 4 =

   $2.34 × 8 =

   $2.34 × 16 =

   $2.34 × 32 =

2. $7,875 ÷ 35 =

   $14,945 ÷ 35 =

   $18,620 ÷ 35 =

   $38,990 ÷ 35 =

3. What is the function of STO ?

4. How do you retrieve a number stored in memory?

5. How do you perform constant multiplication and division on a TI BA-35 Solar calculator?

6. How can you set the BA-35 Solar calculator for a two-decimal place answer?

7. Write the percentage formula.

8. When you know the percentage and the base, how do you find the rate?

For *constant division*, the constant factor is the second number (the divisor) entered and it is also the number to be stored and recalled.

The demonstration problem from page 50 is shown at the right. For a two-decimal place answer, press 2nd [Fix] and enter 2.

2nd [Fix] 2

Annual Salary		Constant Divisor		Weekly Salary
$17,220	÷	52	=	$331.15
$22,140	÷	52	=	$425.77
$25,630	÷	52	=	$492.88
$28,400	÷	52	=	$546.15
$33,390	÷	52	=	$642.12

Enter 52 and store. Enter 17,220, divide, and recall 52. Press the equals key and the result is 331.15.

52 STO 17220 ÷ RCL 2nd [MEM] = 331.15

Enter 22,140, divide, and recall 52. Press the equals key and the result is 425.77.

22140 ÷ RCL 2nd [MEM] = 425.77

Repeat this process of entering each annual salary amount and ÷ , recalling 52 from storage, and pressing = to get each weekly salary.

Practice Test 2

Problems 1 through 25 are a review of Lessons 8 through 12. Estimate answers to Problems 1 through 25.

Use constant multiplication or constant division in Problems 1 through 10.

Use continuous multiplication in Problems 11 through 15. Use the required number of decimal places.

Record your answers on the Answer Tab for Practice Test 2 at the back of the book.

1. $2.75 $\times$ 8 = _____

2. $2.75 $\times$ 22 = _____

3. $2.75 $\times$ 16 = _____

4. $2.75 $\times$ 24.5 = _____

5. $2.75 $\times$ 37.5 = _____

6. $13,080 $\div$ 52 = _____

7. $13,416 $\div$ 52 = _____

8. $13,752 $\div$ 52 = _____

9. $14,088 $\div$ 52 = _____

10. $14,500 $\div$ 52 = _____

11. 42 $\times$ 18 $\times$ 75 = _____

12. 9.4 $\times$ 3.6 $\times$ 5.44 = _____

13. 34 $\times$ 27 $\times$ 2.36 = _____

14. 120 $\times$ 15.8 $\times$ .6783 = _____

15. 68 $\times$ 19.35 $\times$ 2.5436 = _____

Use accumulative multiplication to find the totals in Problems 16 through 19.

Use the required number of decimal places in Problems 16 through 25.

Record your answers on the Answer Tab for Practice Test 2.

After you have completed Practice Test 2, check with your instructor about taking Test 2.

16. $25 \times 25 =$ _____

$36 \times 42 =$ _____

$239 \times 99 =$ _____

_____ T

17. $\$17.79 \times 9 =$ _____

$\$5.99 \times 17 =$ _____

$\$25.98 \times 6 =$ _____

$\$10.98 \times 5.5 =$ _____

$=$ _____ T

18. $15 \times \$7.50 =$ _____

$18 \times \$10.75 =$ _____

$17 \times \$19.95 =$ _____

_____ T

19. $325 \times 108.1 =$ _____

$236 \times 94.25 -$ _____

$111.1 \times 225.55 =$ _____

_____ T

20. $(85 \times 75) + (65 \times 49) =$ _____

21. $(278.5 \times 503.5) + (172.4 \times 40.44) =$ _____

22. $(4 \times \$12.98) - (2 \times \$6.75) = \$$_____

23. $(12 \times \$4.75) - (6 \times \$2.38) = \$$_____

24. $(8 \times \$19.98) + (3 \times \$10.95) = \$$_____

25. $(24 \times \$2.39) - (12 \times \$1.99) = \$$_____

L E S S O N 13

FRACTIONS AND DECIMALS

OBJECTIVES

- *Write business fractions.*
- *Change fractions to decimals.*
- *Calculate with fractions changed to decimals.*
- *Complete Progress Test 6 within 10 minutes and without errors.*

FRACTIONS

Fractions compare numbers. The terms of a fraction are separated by a line. The fraction 25,000/100,000 means *25,000 out of 100,000.* The top term (**numerator**) of a fraction is compared with the bottom term (**base,** or **denominator**).

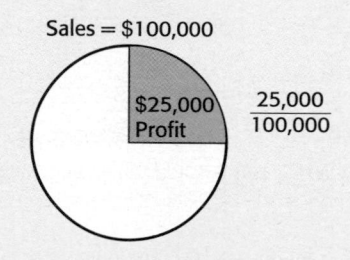

Sales = $100,000

$25,000 Profit

$$\frac{25,000}{100,000}$$

Profit is what fraction *of sales?*

The circle graph to the left shows that profit is compared with sales. Sales is the base, or whole, amount. The base usually follows the word *of.*

Demonstration Problem

Profit is what fraction of sales? Sales = $100,000
Profit = $25,000

SOLUTION: Profit is being compared with sales. Put profit over sales:

$$\text{Profit is } \frac{\$25,000}{\$100,000} \text{ of sales.}$$

This fraction can be reduced to its lowest terms by dividing the numerator (25,000) and denominator (100,000) by the greatest common factor (gcf). The gcf of 25,000 is 25,000.

$$\frac{25,000}{100,000} \div \frac{25,000}{25,000} = \frac{1}{4}$$

A. A deposit of $10,000 earned $480 interest in one year. The interest was what fraction *of the deposit?*

$$\text{ANSWER: Interest} \div \text{Deposit} = \frac{\$480}{\$10,000} \div \frac{80}{80} = \frac{6}{125}$$

The numerator may be **larger** than the denominator. Remember, the denominator is the amount that follows *of*.

Demonstration Problem

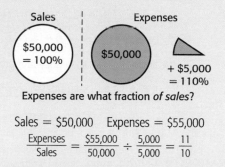

Sales   Expenses

$50,000 = 100%

$50,000

+ $5,000 = 110%

Expenses are what fraction *of sales*?

Sales = $50,000   Expenses = $55,000

$$\frac{\text{Expenses}}{\text{Sales}} = \frac{\$55,000}{50,000} \div \frac{5,000}{5,000} = \frac{11}{10}$$

Expenses were compared with sales. Sales is the base of comparison, even though it is the smaller number. (In this case, the company lost money.)

Check Problems A and B before answering Problems 1 through 7. Record your answers on the Answer Tab for Lesson 13.

B. A lottery ticket cost $2 and paid off $151. The payoff was what fraction *of the ticket's cost*?

ANSWER: Payoff ÷ Cost = $\dfrac{\$151}{\$2}$

Write the fraction in lowest terms for each problem. No calculator is needed.

1. A jacket that usually sells for $100 is marked $20 off. The amount off is what fraction of the usual price?

2. A bank deposit of $300 earned $9 interest. The interest was what fraction of the deposit?

3. Of the 100 people who tested three sodas, 60 people preferred soda A. What fraction of the people preferred soda A?

4. Last year's profit was $300,000. This year's profit was $400,000. This year's profit is what fraction of last year's profit?

5. A business could not collect $5,000 that it was owed. The total owed to the business was $100,000. What fraction of the total was not collected?

6. A company that owed $2,000 paid early and got a $40 discount. What fraction of the amount owed was the discount?

7. A house bought for $70,000 was sold for $105,000. The selling price was what fraction of the purchase price (cost)?

DECIMALS

A decimal is a kind of fraction. The decimal .5 means 5 tenths, or $\frac{5}{10}$. Any fraction can be made into a decimal equivalent by dividing the numerator by the denominator.

C. $\frac{1,480}{10,000} = (1,480 \div 10,000) = .148$

If the numerator is larger than the denominator, then the decimal equivalent will be greater than 1.

D. $\frac{151}{2} = (151 \div 2) = 75.5$

To change a mixed number into a decimal, just change the fraction and attach its decimal value to the whole number.

E. $\frac{1}{2} = .5$, and therefore $3\frac{1}{2} = 3.5$

Round repeating decimals to five places.

F. $\frac{6}{9} = 6 \div 9 = .6666666666 = .66667$

Check Problems C through F.

To round fractions, round to the nearest whole. If the fraction is $\frac{1}{2}$ or greater, round up. If the fraction is less than $\frac{1}{2}$, round down to the nearest whole number.

Fractions are often hard to compare, but decimals are obvious. Use your calculator to change each pair of fractions into decimal equivalents. Write the larger values for Problems 8 through 15 on the Answer Tab for Lesson 13. Check Problem G first. The larger value for Problem G is circled.

G. Which fraction is larger, $\frac{65}{128}$ or $\frac{73}{140}$?

ANSWER: $\frac{65}{128} = .50781$ $\qquad$ $\frac{73}{140} = \boxed{.52143}$

Which value is larger? If the fractions are equal, write equal on the Answer Tab.

8. $\frac{6}{95}$ or $\frac{6}{96}$?

9. $\frac{13}{100}$ or $\frac{7}{50}$?

10. $\frac{73}{67}$ or $\frac{37}{34}$?

11. $\frac{362}{158}$ or $\frac{758}{170}$?

12. $\frac{6}{8}$ or $\frac{7}{9}$?

13. $31\frac{5}{8}$ or $31\frac{48}{75}$?

14. $\frac{50}{85}$ or $\frac{43}{78}$?

15. $\frac{16}{32}$ or $\frac{51}{102}$?

CALCULATING WITH FRACTIONS

Decimal equivalents are also used to add, subtract, multiply, or divide on the calculator. Change the fractions into decimals and calculate as usual. Estimate your answer first.

H. Problem: $2\frac{5}{6}$ $+$ $10\frac{4}{9}$ $-$ $1\frac{1}{8}$ $=$? Estimate: $3 + 10 - 1 = 12$

ANSWER: 2.83333 $+$ 10.44444 $-$ 1.125 $=$ 12.15277 The answer is reasonable.

I. Problem: $\frac{33}{5}$ $\times$ $4\frac{5}{8}$ $\div$ $6\frac{1}{4}$ $=$? Estimate: $6 \times 5 \div 6 = 5$

ANSWER: 6.6 $\times$ 4.625 $\div$ 6.25 $=$ 4.884 The answer is reasonable.

Memorizing the decimal equivalents of the most common fractions will save you time when calculating with fractions.

FRACTIONS AND THEIR EQUIVALENTS

More Common		Less Common	
$\frac{1}{2}$	= .5	$\frac{1}{6}$	= .16667
$\frac{1}{4}$	= .25	$\frac{5}{6}$	= .83333
$\frac{3}{4}$	= .75	$\frac{1}{8}$	= .125
$\frac{1}{3}$	= .33333	$\frac{3}{8}$	= .375
$\frac{2}{3}$	= .66667	$\frac{5}{8}$	= .625
$\frac{1}{5}$	= .2	$\frac{7}{8}$	= .875
$\frac{2}{5}$	= .4	$\frac{1}{12}$	= .08333
$\frac{3}{5}$	= .6	$\frac{5}{12}$	= .41667
$\frac{4}{5}$	= .8	$\frac{7}{12}$	= .58333
		$\frac{11}{12}$	= .91667

Check Problems H and I. Estimate. Then record your answers to Problems 16 through 25 on the Answer Tab for Lesson 13. Round decimals to five places.

16. $47\frac{11}{12}$ + $79\frac{5}{6}$ − $35\frac{7}{12}$ − $54\frac{1}{3}$ = _____

17. $357\frac{5}{16}$ + $265\frac{7}{8}$ − $245\frac{15}{16}$ − $206\frac{3}{16}$ = _____

18. $35\frac{3}{4}$ + $26\frac{1}{3}$ + $37\frac{5}{6}$ − $29\frac{1}{8}$ = _____

19. $98\frac{5}{12}$ − $46\frac{1}{6}$ + $22\frac{2}{3}$ − $16\frac{1}{12}$ = _____

20. $78\frac{3}{4}$ + $95\frac{4}{5}$ − $36\frac{1}{3}$ − $12\frac{5}{6}$ = _____

21. $12\frac{1}{2}$ × $54\frac{1}{4}$ ÷ $55\frac{5}{8}$ = _____

22. $12\frac{4}{9}$ × $7\frac{3}{8}$ ÷ $6\frac{1}{5}$ = _____

23. $18\frac{4}{15}$ × $36\frac{7}{16}$ × $2\frac{2}{5}$ ÷ $38\frac{5}{9}$ = _____

24. $30\frac{1}{3}$ × $9\frac{5}{7}$ × $3\frac{3}{32}$ ÷ $41\frac{3}{5}$ = _____

25. $17\frac{5}{13}$ × $3\frac{7}{15}$ × $5\frac{3}{4}$ ÷ $24\frac{1}{4}$ = _____

Business Application 1

Part of a payroll register is shown to the right. Change all fractions to decimals. Round decimals to five places. Multiply the number of hours worked by the hourly rate to find the gross pay.

Estimate $38\frac{1}{4} \times 5.88$ as $40 \times 6 = 240$. Compared to the estimate, the answer is reasonable.

Set the Decimal Point Selector at two. Express money amounts to the nearest cent.

Check Problems J and K. Estimate. Then work Problems 26 through 35. Record your answers on the Answer Tab for Lesson 13.

PAYROLL REGISTER

Employee	Hours Worked	Hourly Rate	Gross Pay	
E. Allan	$38\frac{1}{4}$	$5.88	$ 224.91	J.
C. Crane	$39\frac{3}{4}$	$6.24\frac{1}{2}$	$ 248.24	K.
T. Engel	$37\frac{1}{2}$	$6.75	$	26.
F. Farnsworth	$38\frac{1}{3}$	$6.87\frac{1}{2}$	$	27.
S. Guadalupe	39	$5.37\frac{1}{2}$	$	28.
L. Lopez	$37\frac{2}{3}$	$6.55	$	29.
C. Ming	38	$6.25\frac{1}{2}$	$	30.
C. Ngo	$38\frac{5}{6}$	$6.38	$	31.
D. Pei	$39\frac{1}{4}$	$6.98	$	32.
J. Reyes	$37\frac{1}{3}$	$7.25	$	33.
K. Rodriquez	$38\frac{3}{4}$	$7.75	$	34.
I. Thomas	$38\frac{1}{2}$	$7.87\frac{1}{2}$	$	35.

Business Application 2

Very often businesses and individuals invest earnings and savings in stocks and bonds. These are often temporary investments because they can be sold at any time. Stock prices are quoted to the nearest eighth of a dollar. Bonds are also quoted as fractional amounts. See Lesson 26 for examples of stock prices and Lesson 27 for examples of bond prices.

Extend the total cost of each investment listed to the right. Change fractions to decimals. Multiply the number of shares or bonds by the unit cost. Set the Decimal Point Selector at two. Check Problems L and M. Estimate and work Problems 36 through 45. Record your answers on the Answer Tab for Lesson 13.

After you complete Lesson 13, check with your instructor about taking Progress Test 6 on pages 228 and 229.

TEMPORARY INVESTMENTS

Number of Shares	Name of Stock	Unit Cost	Total	
125	Bell Motors Corporation	$53.87\frac{1}{2}$	$ ___6,734.38___	**L.**
150	General Container Corp.	$36.62\frac{1}{2}$	$ _____	**36.**
225	Business Machines Company	$57.37\frac{1}{2}$	$ _____	**37.**
1,250	A. P. Electronics Inc.	$15.12\frac{1}{2}$	$ _____	**38.**
133	Pollution Controls Inc.	$12.87\frac{1}{2}$	$ _____	**39.**
317	Rogers Restaurant Corp.	$13.62\frac{1}{2}$	$ _____	**40.**

Number of Bonds	Issued by	Unit Cost	Total	
7	U.S. government	$1,000.93\frac{3}{4}$	$ ___7,006.56___	**M.**
3	U.S. government	$ 999.96\frac{7}{8}$	$ _____	**41.**
5	U.S. government	$ 984.37\frac{1}{2}$	$ _____	**42.**
6	U.S. government	$ 807.65\frac{5}{8}$	$ _____	**43.**
3	U.S. government	$1,024.68\frac{3}{4}$	$ _____	**44.**
9	U.S. government	$ 992.81\frac{1}{4}$	$ _____	**45.**

LESSON 14

PERCENTS

Percent means hundredths, or parts in 100. The symbol used to express percent is %. A number to the left of the percent symbol indicates the parts of 100. Thus, 25% means 25 parts of 100, written as the fraction $\frac{25}{100}$, or 25 divided by 100. Percents are expressed as decimals on the calculator.

Demonstration Problem

$$25\% = ?\ \text{decimal}$$

$$25\% = .25$$

$$1\tfrac{1}{2}\% = ?\ \text{decimal}$$

$$1\tfrac{1}{2}\% = 1.5\% = .015$$

To change a percent to a decimal, divide the number by 100. For instance, 25% equals 25 divided by 100, which equals .25.

$$100\overline{)25.00}\quad\begin{array}{c}.25\end{array}\quad 25\% = .25$$

A shortcut to change a percent to a decimal is to drop the percent sign and move the decimal point two places to the left.

$$25\% = 25.\% = .25.\% = .25$$

Remember that there is a decimal point to the right of any whole number.

To change a *mixed number percent* such as $1\tfrac{1}{2}\%$ to decimal form, first make the mixed number a decimal percent. Then change the percent to a decimal (divide by 100).

$$\text{First } 1\tfrac{1}{2}\% = 1.5\%\quad\text{Then } 1.5\% = .01.5\% = .015$$

Dividing 1.5 by 100 meant moving the decimal point two places to the left. A zero was inserted for the place value of thousandths.

CHANGING DECIMALS TO PERCENTS

Decimals are changed to percents to make them easier to talk about. Simply multiply the decimal by 100 (or move the decimal point two places to the right) and attach a percent symbol (%). Since the percent symbol means divided by 100, it cancels the effect of multiplying by 100. The value of the percent will be exactly the same as the decimal.

Demonstration Problems

$.01\frac{1}{4} = .0125 \times 100\% = 1.25\%$ (multiply)

or

$.375 = 37.5\% = 37.5\%$ (move the decimal point two places to the right)

REMEMBER: Make any fraction into a decimal before changing it to a percent.

Record your answers for Problems 1 through 36 on the Answer Tab for Lesson 14.

Check Problems A through C. Then change the following decimals to percents in Problems 1 through 12.

A. $.15 = 15\%$ **B.** $1\frac{1}{3} = 133.33\%$ **C.** $.0001 = .01\%$

1. .0185	**4.** 2.00	**7.** 1	**10.** .875
2. 2.732	**5.** .625	**8.** $.6\frac{2}{3}$	**11.** .005
3. .0042	**6.** $.83\frac{1}{3}$	**9.** .29	**12.** $.6\frac{1}{4}$

Check Problems D through F. Then change the following percents to decimals.

D. $350\% = 3.5$ **E.** $.07\% = .0007$ **F.** $27\frac{1}{2}\% = .275$

13. 28.6%	**16.** .04%	**19.** .6%	**22.** 125%
14. 165.4%	**17.** 13.5%	**20.** .06%	**23.** 12.5%
15. .84%	**18.** 8.4%	**21.** .006%	**24.** 1.25%

Change the following decimals to percents and percents to decimals.

25. $.87\frac{1}{2}$	**28.** $133\frac{1}{3}\%$	**31.** 12.5	**34.** $8\frac{1}{3}\%$
26. 1.75	**29.** 66%	**32.** 1.5	**35.** $37\frac{1}{2}\%$
27. $.06\frac{1}{4}$	**30.** $16\frac{2}{3}\%$	**33.** .005	**36.** .7%

FRACTIONS TO DECIMALS TO PERCENTS

The relationship between two numbers can be shown as a fraction, decimal, or percent. First, write the fraction. Then change it to a decimal or a percent.

Demonstration Problem

Shoes that usually sell for $50 are marked $10 off. What fraction, decimal, and percent of the usual price is the amount off?

The amount off is $\frac{10}{50}$ of the usual price.

$$\frac{10}{50} = 10 \div 50 = .2 = 20\%$$

The amount off is .2 of the usual price or 20% of the usual price.

NOTE: When the top number in a fraction is larger than the base, the decimal is larger than 1.0 and the percent is larger than 100%.

Check Problem G and work Problems 37 through 45. Record your answers on the Answer Tab for Lesson 14.

For each problem, write the answer as a fraction, a decimal, and a percent.

G. The price of a car went up to $14,500. The old price was $12,500. What fraction of the old price was the new price?

SOLUTION: (fraction) $\frac{14,500}{12,500}$ (decimal) $\underline{1.16}$ (percent) $\underline{116\%}$

37. A real estate agent earned a $7,800 commission on the sale of a $120,000 house. What fraction of the selling price was the agent's commission?

38. In a class of 25 students, there were 10 girls. What fraction of the total class were girls?

39. Last month's sales were $250,000. This month's sales are $300,000. This month's sales are what fraction of last month's sales?

40. A bicycle that usually sells for $200 is marked $25 off. What fraction of the usual price is the amount off?

41. A $3 tip is what fraction of a $20 restaurant bill?

42. There was a $45 finance charge on a $3,000 bill. What fraction of the total bill was the finance charge?

43. A company received a $30 discount on a $1,000 invoice. What fraction of the invoice was the discount?

44. A business has accounts receivable of $50,000. What fraction of accounts receivable is an uncollectible account of $750?

45. A business owes $400 interest on a one-year note for $5,000. What fraction of the note is owed for interest?

FRACTION, DECIMAL, AND PERCENT REVIEW

Demonstration Problem

The fraction $\frac{1}{12}$ is equal to what decimal and what percent?

$$1 \div 12 = .08333$$

$$\frac{1}{12} = 8.333\% \text{ or } 8\frac{1}{3}\%$$

Check Problems H through K. Fill in the missing blanks, indicating the equivalent fraction, decimal, or percent. Record your answers for Problems 46 through 67 on the Answer Tab for Lesson 14. (Carry decimals to five places.)

Fractions		Decimals		Percents	
$\frac{1}{3}$		.33333	H.	$33\frac{1}{3}\%$	I.
$\frac{5}{8}$	J.	.625		62.5%	K.
$\frac{7}{12}$			46.		47.
$\frac{3}{16}$			48.		49.
	50.		51.	$66\frac{2}{3}\%$	
	52.	.875			53.
	54.		55.	$37\frac{1}{2}\%$	
$\frac{1}{16}$			56.		57.
$\frac{1}{40}$			58.		59.
$\frac{3}{5}$			60.		61.
	62.	.8			63.
$\frac{3}{12}$			64.		65.

66. Communication What is the shortcut method for changing a decimal to a percent?

67. Communication What is the shortcut method for changing a percent to a decimal?

FINDING PERCENTAGE, RATE, AND BASE

PERCENTAGE = RATE × BASE

A **percent** compares an amount with a base. The percent is the **rate,** such as a 4% sales tax rate. The **base** is the amount that the rate is applied to, such as a total sale to be taxed. Multiplying the rate by the base gives the **percentage,** such as the amount of tax on a sale.

Demonstration Problem

What is 4% of a $40 sale?

$$\text{Percentage} = \text{Rate} \times \text{Base}$$
$$\$1.60 = .04 \times \$40$$

To find the percentage, change the rate (percent) to a decimal and multiply it by the base. The 4% tax on $60 (.04 × $60) = $2.40.

4% of $40   4% of $60

= $1.60   = $2.40

The percentage gets bigger if the base gets bigger. The 4% sales tax on $60 is more than the 4% sales tax on $40.

Check Problems A and B.

A. Find the 15% discount on a $75 jacket.

Estimate: .20 × 70 = 14.00

.15 × $75.00 = $11.25   discount

An easy way to remember the percentage formula is to show the parts in a triangle.

Percentage = *P*; rate = *R*; base = *B*

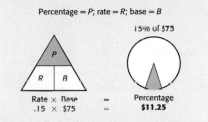

Rate × Base   =   Percentage
.15 × $75   =   **$11.25**

Solving for *P* will tell what the shaded area is worth, or the value of 15% of $75.

B. Find $3\frac{3}{4}$% annual interest on a savings account balance of $254.28.

Estimate: .04 × 250 = 10.00

.0375 × $254.28 = $9.54   interest

(Round money amounts to the nearest cent.)

Estimate. Then answer Problems 1 through 12. Record your answers on the Answer Tab for Lesson 15.

1. What is 35% of $119.21?

2. 5% of $375.25 is _____.

3. $7\frac{1}{2}$% of $1,025.63 is _____.

4. What is $6\frac{1}{4}$% of $8,992?

5. What is $12\frac{1}{8}$% of $1,232.88?

6. The utility company was given permission to charge a temporary 11 32% surcharge. What is the surcharge on a bill of $32.07?

7. The utility company charges a 2% late-payment fee for unpaid bills. What is the charge on an unpaid bill of $40.93?

8. During a $33\frac{1}{3}$%-off sale, how much is taken off the price of a $69.99 digital clock radio?

9. An employee who earns $550.00 per week will receive a $5\frac{1}{2}$% pay raise next week. What is the amount of the pay raise?

10. A real estate agent's commission is 6% of the selling price. What is the commission on a home selling for $138,000?

11. A business estimates that it will not collect $2\frac{1}{4}$% of its credit accounts, which total $75,689.82. What is the amount it will probably not collect?

12. A $1\frac{1}{2}$% cash discount is allowed on an invoice of $1,235.97. What is the amount of the discount?

FINDING THE RATE

The rate shows what fraction the percentage is of the base. This can be done by restating the formula, which can be expressed as Rate = Percentage ÷ Base. (HINT: The number following *of* is the base.)

What percent of 96 is 72?

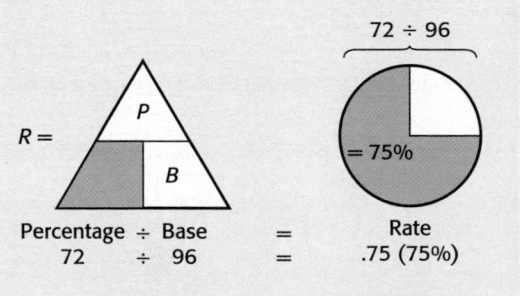

72 ÷ 96

= 75%

Percentage	÷	Base	=	Rate
72	÷	96	=	.75 (75%)

Cover the letter to be found in the triangle. Covering the *R* leaves the fraction *P/B*. The triangle shows:

$$\text{Rate} = \frac{\text{Percentage}}{\text{Base}}, \text{ or } R = P \div B$$

Demonstration Problem

What percent of 96 is 72?

1. Estimate: $R = 70 \div 100 = \frac{70}{100}$ or 70%.

2. Clear. Set the Decimal Point Selector at four; set the Round switch at the five/four position.

3. Write the fraction: $\text{Rate} = \frac{\text{Percentage}}{\text{Base}} = \frac{72}{96}$.

4. Solve.

Enter	Press	Tape
	T	0.0000 T
72	÷	72.0000 ÷
96	=	96.0000 =
		.7500

Compared to the estimate, the answer is reasonable.

5. Change the decimal to a percent: Rate = .75 = 75%.
   ANSWER: 72 is 75% of 96.

Check Problems C and D. Then estimate and solve Problems 13 through 17. Set the Decimal Point Selector at four. Record your answers on the Answer Tab for Lesson 15.

C. Profit = $12.48; cost = $74.88. Profit was what percent of cost?   <u>16.67%</u>

D. Your sales equal $.95 million. Their sales are $1.5 million. Your sales are what percent of their sales?   <u>63.33%</u>

13. What percent of 8 is 7?

14. What percent of 8 is 12?

15. If $1,200 is returned on an investment of $950, what percent of the investment was the return?

16. A school has a student population of 1,679. Of this number, 897 are boys. Boys make up what percent of the student body?

17. A store's daily sales totaled $60,000. The sales of the store's four departments were A: $16,000; B: $8,000; C: $12,000; and D: $24,000. Find each department's percent of the total sales. (HINT: As a check on your work, total the percents. The total should equal 100%.) Round to the nearest hundredth.

FINDING THE BASE

The base can be found when the rate (%) and the percentage are known.

Use the percentage formula, $B = \frac{P}{R}$. Divide the percentage by the rate.

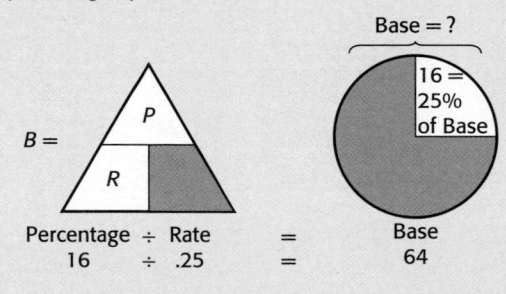

Base = ?

16 = 25% of Base

$B =$

P

R

Percentage ÷ Rate = Base
16 ÷ .25 = 64

Demonstration Problem

The number 16 equals 25% of what number?

Estimate: $20 \div .30 \approx 66$

Base = Percentage ÷ Rate
64 = 16 ÷ 25%

CHECK: Does 25% × 64 = 16?   Yes

When looking for the base, divide the percentage by the rate. Remember to change the rate (percent) to a decimal before you divide. Check Problems E through G. Estimate and record your answers to Problems 18 through 25 on the Answer Tab for Lesson 15. (HINT: The number following *of* is the base.) Check your work as shown in the Demonstration Problem.

E. 6 is 15% of what number? $6 \div .15 = \underline{\ 40\ }$

F. 118% of what number equals $5.40? $\$5.40 \div 1.18 = \underline{\ \$4.58\ }$

G. 375 is $62\frac{1}{2}$% of what number? $375 \div .625 = \underline{\ 600\ }$

18. 30 is 25% of what number?

19. 4% of what number equals $4.36?

20. $130.00 is $12\frac{1}{2}$% of what amount?

21. $153.00 is 17% of what amount?

22. 150% of what number equals 300?

23. 248 is 5% of what number?

24. If a 5% commission on daily sales amounted to $54.50, what was the amount of the sales?

25. If the 15% down payment on a house amounted to $13,500, what was the price of the house?

REVIEW OF PERCENTAGE, RATE, AND BASE

$$Percentage = Rate \times Base$$

$$Rate = \frac{Percentage}{Base}$$

$$Base = \frac{Percentage}{Rate}$$

(HINT: The number following *of* is the base.)
Estimate and work Problems 26 through 36 and record your answers on the Answer Tab for Lesson 15. Round your answers to two decimal places.

To check your work, place your answer back into the question. Does your answer make sense?

26. What is $37\frac{1}{2}$% of 144?   **Estimate:** $.4 \times 140 = 56.0$

27. What is 4% of 172.5?

28. $133\frac{1}{3}$% of what amount is $64?

29. What percent of $300 is $50?

30. $31.62 is 8% of what amount?

31. Last year's profits were $288,000. This year's profits dropped to $264,000. This year's profits are what percent of last year's profits?

32. The profits of a business are $30,000. Maria Ruiz receives 40% of the profits. What amount does Ms. Ruiz receive?

33. If a baseball team owner gets $95,863 of the $798,858 collected by concessions, what percent of the concessions does the owner get?

34. John Reed's gross salary is $351.20. His deductions total $52.68. What percent of his salary is for deductions?

35. If the 5% sales tax on a store's receipts for one day amounted to $235.65, what were the receipts on which the sales taxes were figured?

36. Communication   State the three forms of the percentage formula.

AMOUNTS AND PERCENTS OF INCREASE OR DECREASE

Business people compare amounts such as sales, expenses, or profit from time to time. The amount and percent of change can show a business's progress. Subtract the old amount from the new amount to find the increase or decrease. Then divide by the old amount to find the *percent* of increase or decrease.

The graph shows an increase in sales from last year to this year.

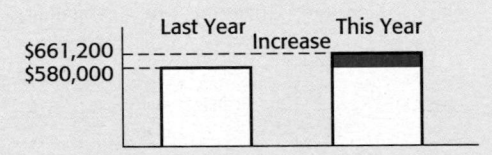

Sales

Demonstration Problem

Sales this year totaled $661,200. Last year's sales totaled $580,000 What is the amount and percent of increase?

1. Clear. Set the Decimal Point Selector at four and the Round switch at five/four.

2. Solve. Percent of increase = (New − Old) ÷ Old.

Enter	Press	Tape	
	T	0.0000 T	
661,200	+	661,200.0000 +	Estimate:
580,000	−	580,000.0000 −	700,000 − 600,000 = 100,000
	T	81,200.0000 T	(amount of increase)
	÷	81,200.0000 ÷	Estimate:
580,000	=	580,000.0000 =	100,000 ÷ 600,000 ≈ 16%
		0.1400	(rate of increase)

3. Amount of increase = $81,200. Percent of increase = 14%.

When finding a percent of increase or decrease, the old amount is the base of comparison. The increase or decrease is the amount being compared. When the old is larger than the new, the difference will be negative. The tape calculator will show negative amounts with a minus sign (−) or a CR, or in red. Divide the negative difference by the old amount. The negative decimal equals the percent of decrease.

The graph shows a decrease in price from the old price to the new one.

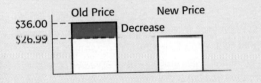

Demonstration Problem

A pair of slacks that once cost $36.00 was marked down to $26.99. What is the amount and percent of decrease?

1. Clear. Set the Decimal Point Selector at four and the Round switch at five/four.

2. Solve. Percent of decrease = (New − Old) ÷ Old. Results will be a negative amount and a rate of decrease.

Enter	Press	Tape	
	T	0.0000 T	
26.99	+	26.9900 +	Estimate:
36.00	−	36.0000 −	40 − 30 = 10
	T	9.0100 T	(amount of decrease)
	÷	−9.0100 ÷	Estimate:
36.00	=	36.0000 =	10 ÷ 40 = 25%
		−0.2503	(rate of decrease)

3. Amount of decrease = $9.01. Percent of decrease = 25.03%.

Business Application 1

An **income statement** is a financial statement that shows the revenues, costs, gross profit, expenses, and the net income or loss of a business during a specified period of time.

A comparison of the amount and percent of change in income statement items for two periods is called **horizontal analysis.**

Estimate. Then find the amount and the percent of increase or decrease in the income statement items in Problems 1 through 10. Check Problem A first. Set the Decimal Point Selector at four. Record your answers on the Answer Tab for Lesson 16.

A.B. DISTRIBUTORS
Comparative Income Statement
For the Years Ended December 31, 20XX and 20XX

	20XX	20XX	Amount of Change	Percent of Change	
Revenue from Sales:					
Sales	$900,000	$800,000	$100,000	12.50%	**A.**
Less: Returns and Allowances	16,000	16,000			**1.**
Net Sales	$884,000	$784,000			**2.**
Cost of Goods Sold	450,000	400,000			**3.**
Gross Profit on Sales	$434,000	$384,000			**4.**
Operating Expenses:					
Selling Expenses	$125,000	$100,000			**5.**
Warehouse Expenses	50,000	50,000			**6.**
Office Expenses	75,000	70,000			**7.**
Miscellaneous Expenses	35,000	30,000			**8.**
Total Operating Expenses	$285,000	$250,000			**9.**
Net Income	$149,000	$134,000			**10.**

Business Application 2

A **balance sheet** is a financial statement that shows the assets, liabilities, and owner's equity on a specific date. **Assets** are the things a business owns. **Liabilities** are the debts a business owes. **Owner's equity** is the difference between total assets and total liabilities. **Equity** is the owner's claim on the assets of the business.

Estimate. Then find the amount and the percent of increase or decrease in the balance sheet items in Problems 11 through 20. Check Problem B first. Set the Decimal Point Selector at four. Record your answers for Problems 11 through 21 on the Answer Tab for Lesson 16.

After you complete Lesson 16, check with your instructor about taking Progress Test 7 on pages 230 and 231.

QUIGG DISTRIBUTORS, LTD.
Comparative Balance Sheet
December 31, 20XX and 20XX

	20XX	20XX	Amount of Change	Percent of Change	
ASSETS					
Current Assets:					
Cash	$153,150	$149,000	$4,150	2.79%	**B.**
Accounts Receivable	28,000	29,000			**11.**
Merchandise Inventory	102,350	95,000			**12.**
Total Current Assets	$283,500	$273,000			**13.**
Fixed Assets	450,000	400,000			**14.**
Total Assets	$733,500	$673,000			**15.**
LIABILITIES					
Current Liabilities	$148,300	$155,000			**16.**
Long-Term Liabilities	255,000	225,000			**17.**
Total Liabilities	$403,300	$380,000			**18.**
OWNER'S EQUITY					
Adam Barry, Capital	330,200	293,000			**19.**
Total Liabilities and Owner's Equity	$733,500	$673,000			**20.**

SINGLE DISCOUNTS

OBJECTIVES

- *Find discount amounts.*
- *Find amounts due after subtracting discounts.*
- *Use the discount's complement to find amounts due.*

A **discount** is a reduction in the price of an item. The **rate of discount** is expressed as a percent. For example, a cash discount of 2% may be granted to a buyer for paying promptly. A **trade discount** of 40% may be given to a retailer for buying in large quantities.

CASH DISCOUNTS. A **cash discount** is offered under conditions called *credit terms*, such as 2/10, *n*/30. The 2/10 means that the buyer may deduct 2% if the invoice is paid within 10 days. The *n*/30 means that the *net* or *full invoice amount* is due within 30 days.

Remember to estimate your answers first.

Demonstration Problem

Find (a) the cash discount available on the invoice below and (b) the amount due if paid by January 25.

Terms: 2/10, *n*/30		Invoice No.:	019508
		Date:	1/15/--
Please Pay		TOTAL:	$2,021.92

1. Clear. Set the Decimal Point Selector at two and the Round switch at five/four.

2.

(Base)		(Rate)		(Percentage)
Invoice Amount		Discount Rate		Discount Amount
$2,021.92	×	.02	=	$ 40.44

3.

Invoice Amount		Discount Amount		Amount Due
$2,021.92	−	$40.44	=	$1,981.48

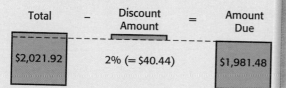

Total − Discount Amount = Amount Due

Total	−	Discount Amount	=	Amount Due
$2,021.92		2% (= $40.44)		$1,981.48

Check Problems A and B before solving Problems 1 through 10.

Total	Discount or Terms	Discount Amt/ Amt Due
$196.20	3%	A. $ 5.89
		A. $ 190.31
$103.39	4/10, n/30	B. $ 4.14
		B. $ 99.25

Record your answers on the Answer Tab for Lesson 17.

Here are two methods of finding the discount amount and the amount due in a continuous operation. Check the features of your calculator.

Method I: Enter the rate as a decimal.

Enter	Press	Tape
	T	0.00 T
2,021.92	+	2,021.92 +
	×	2,021.92 ×
.02	=	.02 =
		40.44 (discount amt)
	−	40.44 −
	T	1,981.48 T (amt due)

Method II: Use the ⊡% key.

Enter	Press	Tape
		0.00 T
2,021.92	×	2,021.91 ×
2	%	2 %
		40.44
	−	1,981.48

For each problem, find (a) the discount amount and (b) the amount due. The cash payment is made within the terms of the discount.

	Total	Discount or Terms		Total	Discount or Terms
1.	$ 385.33	3%	6.	$2,130.35	5/10, n/30
2.	$ 406.77	2/30, n/60	7.	$ 962.19	2%
3.	$ 196.75	2%	8.	$1,188.75	3%
4.	$1,054.13	$2\frac{1}{2}$%	9.	$2,396.00	3/10, n/30
5.	$ 845.40	4/15, n/30	10.	$4,866.04	$1\frac{1}{2}$%

TRADE DISCOUNTS

A **trade discount** is a reduction from the list price of an item. The **list price** is published in the seller's catalog. The list price minus the trade discount equals the net price, which is the price the retailer or buyer pays.

If the seller offers both trade discounts and cash discounts, *the trade discount is always deducted first.*

Work the demonstration problem at the right.

Demonstration Problem

Terms: 3/30, *n*/60		Invoice No. 1234
		April 1, 20–

Quantity	Description	Unit Price	Extension
10	Portable Color TV	$398	$3,980
		Total (List Price)	$3,980
		40% trade discount	1,592
		NET PRICE	$2,388

For the invoice above, find (a) the amount of trade discount, (b) the net price, (c) the amount of cash discount, and (d) the amount due if paid by May 1.

a.
List Price		Rate of Trade Discount		Amount of Trade Discount
$3,980	×	40% (.40)	=	$1,592

b.
List Price		Amount of Trade Discount		Net Price
$3,980	−	$1,592	=	$2,388

c.
Net Price		Rate of Cash Discount		Amount of Cash Discount
$2,388	×	3% (.03)	=	$71.64

d.
Net Price		Amount of Cash Discount		Amount Due
$2,388	−	$71.64	=	$2,316.36

Estimate discounts before calculating to check your work. Divide the price by 100 to find 1%. (Just move the decimal point two places to the left.) Then multiply by the number of percents.

$$3980 \times 40\% = ?$$
(Divide by 100) $\quad 39.80 \times 40 \quad = ?$
(Estimate) $\qquad 40 \times 40 \quad = 1,600$

The exact answer is 1,592, and so your estimate confirms the calculator answer.

Method I: Enter rate as a decimal.

Enter	Press	Tape
	T	0.00 T
3,980	+	3,980.00 +
	×	3,980.00 ×
.40	=	0.40 =
		1592.00 (a)
	−	1,592.00 −
	S	2,388.00 S (b)
	×	2,388.00 ×
.03	=	0.03 =
		71.64 (c)
	−	71.64 −
	T	2,316.36 T (d)

Method II: Use the % **key.**

Enter	Press	Tape
	T	0.00 T
3,980	×	3,980.00 ×
40	%	40.00 %
		1,592.00
	−	2,388.00
	×	2,388.00 ×
3	%	3.00 %
		71.64
	−	2,316.36

List Price		Trade Discount		Net Amount		Cash Discount		Amount Due
	−		=		−		=	
$3,980		$1,592		$2,388		$71.64		$2,316.36

Check Problem C before solving Problems 11 through 20. Record your answers on the Answer Tab for Lesson 17.

USING THE COMPLEMENT OF A DISCOUNT

A discount is subtracted from a price. If a 30% discount is offered, the buyer pays the full price minus 30%. Since the full price is 100%, the buyer pays 100% − 30%, or 70%.

The **complement** of any percent is equal to that percent subtracted from 100%. For example, the complement of 60% is 40%.

Multiply the list price by the discount's complement to find the net price. Work the demonstration problem at the right.

	List Price	Trade Discount Rate	Trade Discount Amount	Net Price	Cash Discount Rate	Cash Discount Amount	Amount Due
C.	$1,800.82	30%	$ 540.25	$ 1,260.57	2%	$ 25.21	$ 1,235.36
11.	$2,000.00	25%	$_____	$_____	2%	$_____	$_____
12.	$5,789.54	35%	$_____	$_____	3%	$_____	$_____
13.	$4,333.65	20%	$_____	$_____	$1\frac{1}{2}$%	$_____	$_____
14.	$8,823.30	15%	$_____	$_____	1%	$_____	$_____
15.	$6,250.00	45%	$_____	$_____	2%	$_____	$_____
16.	$1,975.75	35%	$_____	$_____	5%	$_____	$_____
17.	$2,250.50	40%	$_____	$_____	3%	$_____	$_____
18.	$3,750.75	50%	$_____	$_____	1%	$_____	$_____
19.	$3,450.98	35%	$_____	$_____	4%	$_____	$_____
20.	$5,657.98	30%	$_____	$_____	3%	$_____	$_____

Demonstration Problem

List price, $250; trade discount, 30%. Find the net price.

$$\text{Discount's Complement} = 100\% - \text{Discount}$$
$$70\% = 100\% - 30\%$$
$$\text{Net Price} = \text{List Price} \times \text{Discount's Complement}$$
$$\$175 = \$250 \qquad 70\%$$

Trade Discount 30%

Discount's Complement 70%

List Price 100%

To find the discount amount, multiply the price by the *discount*. To find the amount due, multiply by the *discount's complement*.

NOTE: If both the discount amount and the net price are rounded up, there will be a one cent ($.01) error. In such cases, round the discount amount up and round the net price down.

Check Problem D before solving Problems 21 through 30. Record your answers for Problems 21 through 31 on the Answer Tab for Lesson 17.

For calculators with a Constant Operation mode:

1. Set the calculator for constant multiplication.

2. Enter the price, $250, as the multiplier.

   Multiply by the discount, 30% (.3).

3. Multiply by the discount's complement, 70% (.7).

Tape

250 ×

.3 =

75

.7 =

175

	List Price	Trade Discount	Complement of Trade Discount		Discount Amount	Net Price
D.	$ 250.00	30%	70	%	$ 75.00	$ 175.00
21.	$2,398.20	20%		%	$	$
22.	$9,000.00	40%		%	$	$
23.	$6,423.35	45%		%	$	$
24.	$3,333.50	25%		%	$	$
25.	$1,888.00	20%		%	$	$
26.	$4,387.65	15%		%	$	$
27.	$1,124.50	35%		%	$	$
28.	$6,666.66	30%		%	$	$
29.	$9,909.90	35%		%	$	$

30. **Communication** What is the complement of a trade discount?

LESSON 18

SERIES DISCOUNTS

· ·

Many businesses offer more than one trade discount. A *series discount*, such as 25%, 10% means that 25% is deducted from the list price and 10% is deducted from what is left. (The expression 25%, 10% does *not* mean 35% off.)

The net price on a bill marked $800 less 25%, 10% could be found by taking each discount, one at a time:

$$\$800 - (25\% \text{ of } \$800) = \$600$$

$$\$600 - (10\% \text{ of } \$600) = \$540 \text{ (net amount)}$$

An easier method to find the net amount uses the discounts' complements.

Demonstration Problem

Find the net price due on an invoice marked $800 less 25%, 10%.

1. Find the discounts' complements: $100\% - 25\% = 75\%$; $100\% - 10\% = 90\%$.

2. Multiply the discounts' complements: $.75 \times .90 = .675$

3. Multiply by the list price: $.675 \times 800 = 540$

Enter	Press	Tape
	T	0.00 T
0.75	×	0.75 ×
0.9	×	0.90 ×
800.	=	800.00 =
		540.00 (net price)

OBJECTIVES

- *Find net prices and series discount amounts using discounts' complements.*
- *Use a table to find the single complement of a series discount.*
- *Complete Progress Test 8 within 10 minutes and without errors.*

List price less 25%, 10%

List $800	Complement of First Discount	Complement of Second Discount
100%	75% of 100%	90% of 75% = $540

If a bill is reduced 25%, 10%, the buyer pays 90% of 75% of the bill.

To find the net price with a series of three or more discounts, multiply the list price by each discount's complement.

List $1,200   Discount 20%, 10%, 5%

Net = $1,200 × .8 × .9 × .95
    = $820.80

Remember to estimate your answers first.

Check Problem A. Record your answers for Problems 1 through 10 on the Answer Tab for Lesson 18.

Set the Decimal Point Selector at two and the Round switch in the five/four position.

	List Price	Series Trade Discount	Net Price
A.	$ 721.80	15%, 10%, 10%	$ ___496.96___
1.	$ 453.50	20%, 10%, 10%	$ _____
2.	$ 676.00	10%, 10%	$ _____
3.	$ 499.50	30%, 10%, 5%	$ _____
4.	$ 314.65	25%, 10%, 10%	$ _____
5.	$ 289.50	10%, 5%	$ _____
6.	$1,286.35	25%, 25%, 10%	$ _____
7.	$2,508.08	25%, 10%, $2\frac{1}{2}$%	$ _____
8.	$ 610.00	10%, 10%, 10%, 10%	$ _____
9.	$8,000.00	$22\frac{1}{2}$%, $7\frac{1}{2}$%	$ _____
10.	$1,600.50	10%, 5%, $2\frac{1}{2}$%	$ _____

DISCOUNT AMOUNTS. To find the discount amount with a series discount, find the net and subtract it from the list:

List $2,500   Discount 25%, 10%

Net = $2,500 × .75 × .90
    = $1,687.50

List − Net = Discount
$2,500 − $1,687.50 = $812.50

Check Problem B. Record your answers for Problems 11 through 20 on the Answer Tab for Lesson 18.

NOTE: If both the discount amount and the net price are rounded up, there will be a one cent ($.01) error. In such cases, round the discount amount up and round the net price down.

	List Price	Series Trade Discount	Net Price	Discount Amount
B.	$ 1,250.80	5%, $2\frac{1}{2}$%	$ 1,158.55	$ 92.25
11.	$ 455.50	20%, 10%, 10%	$	$
12.	$ 575.00	10%, 10%, 10%	$	$
13.	$ 895.50	30%, 10%, 5%	$	$
14.	$ 512.65	25%, 10%, 10%	$	$
15.	$ 298.40	10%, 5%, 5%	$	$
16.	$ 766.66	12%, 10%, 8%	$	$
17.	$ 932.04	25%, 25%	$	$
18.	$ 3,960.00	30%, 10%, 2%	$	$
19.	$12,393.28	35%, 20%, 2%	$	$
20.	$ 1,539.13	40%, 5%, 5%	$	$

Business Application

Complete the invoices at the right.

1. Find the net price.

2. Find the trade discount.

3. Take the cash discount on the net price.

4. Find the amount due, if paid according to cash discount terms.

Record your answer for Problems 21 through 32 on the Answer Tab for Lesson 18.

Quantity	Description	Unit Price	Extension	
50	Jackets	$99.95		
	Less Trade Discount 30%, 5%, 5%		$ _____	21.
	Net Price		$ _____	22.
	Cash Discount $2\frac{1}{2}$%		$ _____	23.
	AMOUNT DUE		$ _____	24.
	(in 10 days)			

Quantity	Description	Unit Price	Extension	
144	Printer Ribbons	$5.00		
	Less Trade Discount 25%, 15%, 10%		$ _____	25.
	Net Price		$ _____	26.
	Cash Discount 2%		$ _____	27.
	AMOUNT DUE		$ _____	28.
	(in 10 days)			

Quantity	Description	Unit Price	Extension	
25	Digital Clock Radios	$85.00		
	Less Trade Discount 30%, 15%, 5%		$ _____	29.
	Net Price		$ _____	30.
	Cash Discount $1\frac{1}{2}$%		$ _____	31.
	AMOUNT DUE		$ _____	32.
	(in 10 days)			

TABLE OF SINGLE COMPLEMENTS FOR SERIES DISCOUNTS

A table such as the one shown on the following page is used to find the single complement of a series discount. Use this complement to find discount amounts and net prices. To find the net price for a series discount of 20%, 10%, 5%, do the following:

1. Locate the vertical column labeled 20% and move your eye down the column until you reach the horizontal row labeled 10%, 5%. The number at the intersection of the column and row is .684. The net will be 68.4% of the list.

2. Multiply .684, the single complement for 20%, 10%, 5%, by the list price to find the net price.

Check Problem C and use the table of single complements for series discounts to complete Problems 33 through 41. Record your answers on the Answer Tab for Lesson 18.

	List Price	Series Trade Discount	Series Discount from Table	Net Price
C.	$571.96	$16\frac{2}{3}$%, 10%, 10%	.675	$ 386.07
33.	$659.95	25%, 10%, 10%	_____	$ _____
34.	$493.65	$27\frac{1}{2}$%, 10%	_____	$ _____
35.	$906.75	25%, 10%, 10%, 5%	_____	$ _____
36.	$739.00	30%, 10%, 10%, 5%	_____	$ _____
37.	$450.00	15%, 10%, 5%, $2\frac{1}{2}$%	_____	$ _____

38. Company A sells a radio for $125 less 40% trade discount. Company B sells the same model for $125 less trade discounts of 30% and 10%. Which company has the lower net price?   _____

What will the savings be?   _____

39. Company A sells a TV for $275 less 30% trade discount. Company B sells the same model for $255 less 20% trade discount.

Which company has the lower net price?   _____

What will the savings be?   _____

40. **Communication**   What is the advantage of using a single complement for series discounts?

Rate	5%	7½%	10%	12½%	15%	16⅔%	20%	22½%	25%	27½%	30%	32½%
2½%	.92625	.90188	.8775	.85313	.82875	.8125	.78	.75563	.73125	.70688	.6825	.65813
5%	.9025	.87875	.855	.83125	.8075	.79167	.76	.73625	.7125	.68875	.665	.64125
5%, 2½%	.87994	.85678	.83303	.81047	.78731	.77187	.741	.71784	.69469	.67153	.64838	.62522
5%, 5%	.85738	.83481	.81225	.78969	.76713	.75208	.722	.69944	.67688	.65431	.63175	.60919
5%, 5%, 2½%	.83594	.81394	.79194	.76995	.74795	.73328	.70395	.68195	.65995	.63795	.61596	.59396
7½%	.87875	.85563	.8325	.80938	.78625	.77083	.74	.71688	.69375	.67063	.6475	.62438
7½%, 2½%	.85678	.83423	.81169	.78914	.76659	.75156	.7215	.69895	.67641	.65386	.63131	.60877
7½%, 5%	.83481	.81284	.79088	.76891	.74694	.73229	.703	.68103	.65906	.63709	.61513	.59316
10%	.855	.8325	.81	.7875	.765	.75	.72	.6975	.675	.6525	.63	.6075
10%, 2½%	.83363	.81169	.78975	.76781	.74588	.73125	.702	.68006	.65813	.63619	.61425	.59231
10%, 5%	.81225	.79088	.7695	.74813	.72675	.7125	(.684)	.66263	.64125	.61988	.5985	.57713
10%, 5%, 2½%	.79194	.7711	.75026	.72942	.70858	.69469	.6669	.64606	.62522	.60438	.58354	.56270
10%, 7½%	.79088	.77006	.74925	.72844	.70763	.69375	.666	.64519	.62438	.60356	.58275	.56194
10%, 10%	.7695	.74925	.729	.70875	.6885	.675	.648	.62775	.6075	.58725	.567	.54675
10%, 10%, 5%	.73103	.71179	.69255	.67331	.65408	.64125	.6156	.59636	.57713	.55789	.53865	.51941
10%, 10%, 5%, 2½%	.71275	.69399	.67524	.65648	.63772	.62522	.60021	.58145	.5627	.54394	.52518	.50643
10%, 10%, 10%	.69255	.67433	.6561	.63788	.61965	.6075	.5832	.56498	.54675	.52853	.5103	.49208
10%, 10%, 10%, 10%	.62330	.60689	.59049	.57409	.55769	.54675	.52488	.50848	.49208	.47567	.45927	.44287
10%, 10%, 10%, 10%, 10%	.56097	.54620	.53144	.51668	.50192	.49208	.47239	.45763	.44287	.42811	.41334	.39858

After you complete Lesson 18, check with your instructor about taking Progress Test 8 on pages 232 and 233.

19

EXTENDING INVOICES AND QUANTITY PRICING

OBJECTIVES

- *Extend invoices and find net amount due.*
- *Use quantity pricing (grosses, dozens, hundreds, thousands, reams, and tons).*

EXTENDING INVOICES

Multiplying the quantity of each item on an invoice by its unit price is known as **extending an invoice**. After an invoice is extended, the extension column is added. If there are any trade discounts or sales taxes, they must be subtracted or added, respectively, to find the invoice total.

For all problems in this lesson, set the Decimal Point Selector at two and the Round switch in the five/four position.

Remember to estimate your answer first.

Follow these steps for extending invoices.

1. Use accumulative multiplication (refer to Lesson 11) to extend each item and to find the total for all items sold. Do this in one consecutive operation, as illustrated in the demonstration problem. If your calculator does not have a memory, you must extend each item and then add the extensions to find the total.

2. Compute and deduct any trade discounts from the total to find the net price.

3. Compute and add any sales taxes to find the amount due.

Work the demonstration problem before solving Problems 1 through 14.

Enter	Press	Tape
	T	0.00 T
13	×	13.00 ×
242.00	=+	242.00 = +
		3,146.00 *
40	×	40.00 ×
230.00	=+	230.00 = +
		9,200.00 *
21	×	21.00 ×
170.00	=+	170.00 = +
		3,570.00 *
	*	15,916.00 *
	×	15,916.00 ×
.25	=−	0.25 = −
(discount =)		3,979.00 *
(net price =)	*	11,937.00 *
	×	11,937.00 ×
0.055	=+	0.055 = +
(tax =)		656.54 *
(amount due =)	*	12,593.54 *

Demonstration Problem

DREW & SCOTT SUPPLY HOUSE
11122 Glendale Road
Milwaukee, WI 53201

Invoice No. 35790

Date 9/15/- -

Terms Net

Sold to Winston Barr
1000 Washington Avenue
Chicago, IL 60601

Quantity	Description	Unit Price	Extension
13	5-drawer files	$242.00	$3,146.00
40	4-drawer files	$230.00	$9,200.00
21	2-drawer files	$170.00	$3,570.00
	TOTAL		$15,916.00
	25% trade discount		$ 3,979.00
	Net price		$11,937.00
	5.5% sales tax		$ 656.54
	AMOUNT DUE		$12,593.54

Complete Problems 1 through 14. The problem numbers are placed at the right. Record your answers on the Answer Tab for Lesson 19.

Quantity	Description	Unit Price	Amount	
6	Art files	$114.25	$_____	1.
5	2-drawer file cabinets	$169.75	$_____	2.
3	4-drawer file cabinets	$199.95	$_____	3.
12	Single files	$ 69.50	$_____	4.
12	Card files	$ 16.75	$_____	5.
24	Check files	$ 6.95	$_____	6.
24	Letter files	$136.00	$_____	7.
18	Folder files	$ 14.50	$_____	8.
6	Legal-size file cabinets	$238.75	$_____	9.
		Total	$_____	10.
		30% Trade Discount	$_____	11.
		Net Price	$_____	12.
		6% Sales Tax	$_____	13.
		AMOUNT DUE	$_____	14.

Complete Problems 15 through 26 and record your answers on the Answer Tab for Lesson 19.

Quantity	Description	Unit Price	Amount	
12	Desk pads	$ 37.75	$_____	**15.**
24	Calendars	$ 4.98	$_____	**16.**
36	Letter trays	$ 12.50	$_____	**17.**
24	Letter openers	$ 2.50	$_____	**18.**
8	Desk sets	$ 36.99	$_____	**19.**
6 pr.	Bookends	$ 14.95	$_____	**20.**
6	Wastebaskets	$ 9.75	$_____	**21.**
	Total		$_____	**22.**
	20%, 10%, 10% Trade Discount		$_____	**23.**
	Net Price		$_____	**24.**
	5% Sales Tax		$_____	**25.**
	AMOUNT DUE		$_____	**26.**

EXTENDING ITEMS PRICED BY THE DOZEN AND BY THE GROSS

Some items are priced in quantities rather than as single items. For example, stationery suppliers usually price pencils by the dozen or by the gross.

Demonstration Problems

Quantity		Unit Price		Extension
500	$\times$	$1.50 per dozen	=	?
500	$\times$	$1.50 $\div$ 12	=	$62.50
500	$\times$	$14.40 per gross	=	?
500	$\times$	$14.40 $\div$ 144	=	$50.00

Items priced by the dozen or by the gross can be extended in a continuous operation on your calculator. (Refer to Lesson 10 for mixed operations of multiplication and division.)

To find the extension for an item priced by the dozen, multiply the quantity by the price per dozen. Then divide this amount by the number of units in a dozen (12):

							Tape
500 pencils at $1.50 per dozen		=	?				0.00 T
(500	$\times$	$1.50)	$\div$	12	= $62.50		500.00 $\times$
							1.50 $\div$
							12.00 =
							62.50

Similarly, for an item priced by the gross, divide by the number of units in a gross (144):

500 pencils at $14.40 per gross = ?
(500 $\times$ $14.40) $\div$ 144 = $50.00

Record your answers for Problems 27 through 38 on the Answer Tab for Lesson 19. The problem numbers are on the right.

NOTE: The abbreviations for dozen and gross are **doz.** and **gr.**, respectively.

Quantity	Description	Unit Price	Amount	
100	Erasers	$ 6.00/doz.	$_____	**27.**
75	Soft erasers	$ 4.80/doz.	$_____	**28.**
150	Pencil erasers	$ 3.50/doz.	$_____	**29.**
200	Ink erasers	$ 4.50/doz.	$_____	**30.**
600	Pencils no. 25	$36.00/gr.	$_____	**31.**
300	Permanent markers	$15.50/doz.	$_____	**32.**
300	Fine marking pens	$81.00/gr.	$_____	**33.**
	Total		$_____	**34.**
	20%, 20% Trade Discount		$_____	**35.**
	Net Price		$_____	**36.**
	7% Sales Tax		$_____	**37.**
	AMOUNT DUE		$_____	**38.**

EXTENDING ITEMS PRICED BY THE REAM

Many types of paper used in business offices are sold in **reams** (500 sheets per ream). Memo pads are often sold in packs (pk) of 12.

To find the extension for an item priced by the ream (rm), multiply the quantity times the price per ream and divide by 500, the number of units in a ream.

To find the extension for an item priced in packs of 12, multiply the quantity times the price per pack and divide by 12.

Demonstration Problems

1,500 letterheads at $21.50 per ream = ?
(1,500 × $21.50) ÷ 500 = $64.50

72 legal pads at $10.80 per pack = ?
(72 × $10.80) ÷ 12 = $64.80

Check Problems A and B before solving Problems 39 through 48. Record your answers on the Answer Tab for Lesson 19.

Quantity	Description	Unit Price	Extension	
2,500	Letterheads	$21.75 per rm.	$ 108.75	A.
144	Legal pads (12/pk)	$ 7.35 per pk.	$ 88.20	B.
4,500	Laser print paper	$ 9.75 per rm.	$_____	39.
3,700	No. 8 letterheads	$17.86 per rm.	$_____	40.
5,500	Computer paper	$14.25 per rm.	$_____	41.
2,500	Bond paper (rag content)	$15.75 per rm.	$_____	42.
3,500	Deluxe letterheads	$29.75 per rm.	$_____	43.
500	Colored copy paper	$ 7.75 per rm.	$_____	44.
1,000	Fluorescent copy paper	$14.40 per rm.	$_____	45.
300	Scratch pads	$ 4.50 per pk.	$_____	46.
500	Erasable bond paper	$18.25 per rm.	$_____	47.
48	College ruled pads	$ 9.00 per pk.	$_____	48.

EXTENDING ITEMS PRICED BY THE HUNDRED AND BY THE THOUSAND

To extend items priced by the hundred (per C), use the method described above. Multiply the quantity times the unit price and divide by 100. However, there is a shortcut method. Move the decimal point in the quantity two places to the left and then multiply by the price per 100.

Demonstration Problem

2,500 envelopes at $1.50 per C — ?

2,5.00 × $1.50 = $37.50

To extend items priced by the thousand (per M), move the decimal point in the quantity three places to the left before you multiply.

Check Problems C and D before solving Problems 49 through 59. Record your answers on the Answer Tab for Lesson 19.

Quantity	Description	Unit Price	Extension	
2,500	No. 675 envelopes	$ 1.25 per C	$ __31.25__	C.
2,500	Security envelopes	$13.50 per M	$ __33.75__	D.
5,000	No. 10 envelopes	$ 1.35 per C	$_____	49.
3,000	Self-seal envelopes	$49.90 per M	$_____	50.
7,500	Window envelopes	$17.50 per C	$_____	51.
7,500	Coin envelopes	$36.75 per M	$_____	52.
2,000	Price labels	$ 5.50 per M	$_____	53.
5,000	Mailing labels	$55.75 per M	$_____	54.
2,000	Address labels	$42.25 per M	$_____	55.
1,200	Address labels	$ 4.50 per C	$_____	56.
1,500	#11 manila envelopes	$ 7.75 per C	$_____	57.
1,500	#12 manila envelopes	$37.50 per M	$_____	58.

59. **Communication** What is the proper sequence for finding the amount due for an invoice with a trade discount and a sales tax?

AUDITING INVOICES

OBJECTIVES

- *Audit (check) the extensions and other amounts on invoices.*
- *Complete Progress Test 9 within 10 minutes and without errors.*

Before paying an invoice, the purchaser **audits** (checks) the extensions and other amounts on the invoice. Then the purchaser decides whether it is possible to take advantage of a cash discount if one is offered. If the cash discount is taken, the amount of discount is deducted from the amount due on the invoice. Then a check is written in payment of the invoice.

Work the demonstration problem. The check marks in the audit column indicate that the extension is correct. Incorrect invoice extensions are corrected in the audit column.

Demonstration Problem

TERMS: 2/10, *n*/20   **INVOICE NO. 01950**

Quantity	Description	Unit Price	Extension	Audit
6 doz.	Ball-point pens	$ 15.00/doz.	$ 90.00	✓
12 doz.	Fountain pens	$ 60.00/doz.	$ 720.00	✓
7 doz.	Highlighters	$ 9.50/doz.	$ 66.50	✓
3 gr.	Economy pencils	$ 7.20/gr.	$ 21.60	✓
6 gr.	Medium pencils	$ 11.95/gr.	$ 77.10	$ 71.70
	Total		$ 975.20	$ 969.80
	10% Trade Discount		$ 97.52	$ 96.98
	Net Price		$ 877.68	$ 872.82
	5% Sales Tax		$ 43.88	$ 43.64
	AMOUNT DUE		$ 921.56	$ 916.46

Remember to estimate your answers first.

Set the Decimal Point Selector at two and the Round switch in the five/four position. Then audit the invoices in this lesson. In the audit column at the right, place a check mark next to correct amounts. Write the correct amount next to any incorrect amount.

Record your answers for Problems 1 through 12 on the Answer Tab for Lesson 20.

NOTE: If both the discount amount and the net price are rounded up, there will be a one cent ($.01) error. In such cases, round the discount amount up and round the net price down.

TERMS: 4/10, n/30   **INVOICE NO. 00332**

Quantity	Description	Unit Price	Extension	Audit	
8	Chrome pens	$ 14.78 ea.	$ 118.24	_____	1.
42	Felt tip pens	$ 11.25/doz.	$ 42.88	_____	2.
180	Felt markers	$ 83.00/gr.	$ 103.75	_____	3.
650	Transparent tape	$ 95.50/C	$ 602.75	_____	4.
12,500	Plastic rulers	$ 67.00/M	$ 835.70	_____	5.
3,500	Erasable paper	$ 22.50/rm.	$ 172.50	_____	6.
288	Pocket portfolios	$ 5.25/doz.	$ 162.00	_____	7.
	Total		$2,037.82	_____	8.
	25%, 10% Trade Discount		$ 662.30	_____	9.
	Net Price		$1,375.52	_____	10.
	8% Sales Tax		$ 110.04	_____	11.
	AMOUNT DUE		$1,485.56	_____	12.

Record your answers for Problems 13 through 25 on the Answer Tab for Lesson 20.

TERMS: 3/10, *n*/60   **INVOICE NO. 33036**

Quantity	Description	Unit Price	Extension	Audit	
27 bxs.	Erasable paper	$ 6.00/bx.	$ 210.60	_____	13.
35 bxs.	Bond paper	$ 17.30/bx.	$ 605.50	_____	14.
24 bxs.	Air mail paper	$ 4.00/bx.	$ 96.00	_____	15.
32 bxs.	Laser printing paper	$ 15.70/bx.	$ 504.20	_____	16.
16 bxs.	Recycled bond paper	$ 4.30/bx.	$ 86.80	_____	17.
$3\frac{1}{2}$ gr.	Yellow pencils	$ 25.50/gr.	$ 89.75	_____	18.
$5\frac{1}{4}$ gr.	Colored pencils	$ 29.50/gr.	$ 154.88	_____	19.
$9\frac{1}{2}$ doz.	Marking crayons	$ 3.30/doz.	$ 13.35	_____	20.
		Total	$1,761.08	_____	21.
		22% Trade Discount	$ 387.44	_____	22.
		Net Price	$1,373.64	_____	23.
		5% Sales Tax	$ 68.68	_____	24.
		AMOUNT DUE	$1,442.32	_____	25.

Record your answers for Problems 26 through 38 on the Answer Tab for Lesson 20.

TERMS: $1\frac{1}{2}/10$, $n/30$　　　　　　　　　**INVOICE NO. 27323**

Quantity	Description	Unit Price	Extension	Audit	
14	Halogen desk lamps	$ 29.95	$ 419.00	_____	**26.**
18	Fluorescent lamps	$ 25.95	$ 476.00	_____	**27.**
25	Tensor lamps	$ 18.95	$ 473.75	_____	**28.**
24	No. 7200 desk lamps	$ 39.95	$ 985.80	_____	**29.**
27	No. 9100 desk lamps	$ 66.95	$ 1,708.65	_____	**30.**
20	No. 1500 desk lamps	$ 12.95	$ 259.00	_____	**31.**
18	No. 1600 desk lamps	$ 24.95	$ 449.10	_____	**32.**
125	Halogen bulbs	$ 5.49	$ 696.25	_____	**33.**
Total			$ 5,457.55	_____	**34.**
	25% Trade Discount		$ 1,364.39	_____	**35.**
	Net Price		$ 4,093.16	_____	**36.**
	7% Sales Tax		$ 286.52	_____	**37.**
	AMOUNT DUE		$ 4,379.68	_____	**38.**

Record your answers for Problems 39 through 50 on the Answer Tab for Lesson 20.

TERMS: $2\frac{1}{2}/10$, $n/30$ **INVOICE NO. 17322**

Quantity	Description	Unit Price	Extension	Audit	
9	Bowl mixers	$88.98	$ 800.82	_____	**39.**
11	Waffle griddles	$39.95	$ 439.45	_____	**40.**
4	Electric cookers	$49.50	$ 189.00	_____	**41.**
8	30-cup percolators	$47.25	$ 387.00	_____	**42.**
5	Angus broilers	$43.35	$ 217.65	_____	**43.**
30	Electric can openers	$ 9.95	$ 289.50	_____	**44.**
24	3-speed hand mixers	$17.25	$ 414.00	_____	**45.**
	Total		$2,737.42	_____	**46.**
	25% Trade Discount		$ 684.36	_____	**47.**
	Net Price		$2,053.06	_____	**48.**
	5% Sales Tax		$ 102.65	_____	**49.**
	AMOUNT DUE		$2,155.71	_____	**50.**

Assume that you will pay the invoices in Lesson 20 and can take advantage of the cash discount in each case. Find the cash discount and the actual amount of the check you would write in payment of each invoice. *No cash discount is taken on sales tax.* The cash discount is taken on the net price of the invoice but is deducted from the amount due. Be sure to use the corrected amounts from the audit columns.

Check Problem A and complete Problems 51 through 56. Record your answers on the Answer Tab for Lesson 20.

After completing Lesson 20, check with your instructor about taking Progress Test 9 on pages 234 and 235.

	Invoice No.	Cash Discount	Amount of Check
A.	01950	$ 17.46	$ 899.00
51.	00332	$	$
52.	33036	$	$
53.	27323	$	$
54.	17322	$	$

55. Communication   If an invoice has a trade discount, a cash discount, and a sales tax, give the sequence for finding the net amount of the payment due.

56. Communication   On which amount in Problem 55 is the cash discount taken?

Business Calculator Applications 3

Exercises

Write your response to each question on a separate piece of paper.

Find the percent of increase or decrease. Round to the nearest tenth.

1. 42 new, 36 old

2. 24,000 new, 38,000 old

3. 63 new, 15 old

4. 218,000 new, 346,000 old

Find the percentage, base, or rate.

5. $P = 225, R = 15\%$

6. $B = 328, R = 28\%$

7. $P = 127, B = 508$

Percent of Change, the Percentage Formula, and Discounts

To find the percent of increase or decrease on the TI BA-35 Solar calculator, use the percent change key, 2nd [$\Delta\%$]. If the result is positive, the percent is an increase. If the result is negative, the percent is a decrease. To find the percent of increase or decrease for the demonstration problem on page 100, enter the following.

661,200 2nd [$\Delta\%$] 580,000 = 14

The result is positive so the percent is an increase. The percent of increase is 14%.

The percentage formula is Percentage = Rate × Base, or $P = R \times B$.

To find the base in the demonstration problem on page 94, enter the following.

4 % × 40 = 1.6 or $1.60

To find the rate in the percentage formula, divide the percentage by the base. To find the base, divide the percentage by the rate.

Find the amount due after deducting a cash discount, the trade and cash discounts, and series discounts. Round to the nearest cent.

8. $432.27 total, 2% discount

9. $4,260 list price, 30% trade discount, 2% cash discount

10. $730 less 15%, 8%

Find the net amount due by extending an invoice, getting a total, deducting a trade discount, and adding sales tax. Round to the nearest cent.

11. 12 quantity, $14.00 unit price; 20 quantity, $153.95 unit price; 18 quantity, $22.59 unit price; 20% trade discount, 6.5% sales tax

To find the amount due after deducting a cash discount in the demonstration problem on page 104, enter the following.

$$2,021.92 \boxed{-} 2 \boxed{\%} \boxed{=} 1,981.48$$

To find the trade and cash discounts for the demonstration problem on page 106, enter the following.

$$3,980 \boxed{-} 40 \boxed{\%} \boxed{-} 3 \boxed{\%} \boxed{=} 2,316.36$$

In the demonstration problem for series discounts on page 110, find the complements of the discounts. Enter the following.

$$100 \boxed{-} 25 \boxed{=} 75 \boxed{\%} \boxed{\times} 90 \boxed{\%} \boxed{\times} 800 \boxed{=} 540$$

The demonstration problem on page 117 requires extending an invoice, getting a total, deducting a trade discount, and adding a sales tax. Enter the following.

$$13 \boxed{\times} 242 \boxed{=} \boxed{STO} 40 \boxed{\times} 230 \boxed{=} \boxed{SUM} 21 \boxed{\times} 170 \boxed{=} \boxed{SUM}$$
$$\boxed{RCL} \boxed{2nd} [MEM] \boxed{-} 25 \boxed{\%} \boxed{=} \boxed{+} 5 \boxed{.} 5 \boxed{\%} \boxed{=} 12,593.54$$

Practice Test 3

Problems 1 through 50 are a review of Lessons 13 through 20.

Change the fractions in Problems 1 and 2 to their decimal equivalents. Round to four decimal places in Problems 1 through 8.

Record your answers on the Answer Tab for Practice Test 3 at the back of the book.

1.
$\frac{1}{3} =$ _____

$\frac{2}{3} =$ _____

$\frac{3}{4} =$ _____

$\frac{2}{5} =$ _____

$\frac{5}{7} =$ _____

2.
$\frac{3}{8} =$ _____

$\frac{7}{8} =$ _____

$\frac{4}{9} =$ _____

$\frac{4}{11} =$ _____

$\frac{1}{18} =$ _____

3.
$45\frac{3}{4}$

$34\frac{5}{7}$

$55\frac{1}{3}$

$33\frac{2}{3}$

_____

4.
$107\frac{7}{8}$

$- \ 55$

$- \ 99\frac{4}{9}$

$503\frac{3}{4}$

_____

5. $88\frac{4}{11} \times 24\frac{2}{5} =$ _____

6. $183\frac{7}{8} \times 201\frac{3}{4} =$ _____

7. $999\frac{2}{3} \div 803\frac{1}{3} =$ _____

8. $6{,}666\frac{3}{8} \div 225\frac{1}{18} =$ _____

Complete Problems 9 through 20. Set the Decimal Point Selector at four. Round money amounts to the nearest cent. Express percents to the nearest hundredth. Record your answers on the Answer Tab for Practice Test 3.

9. Find $1\frac{1}{4}\%$ of $4,457.00.

10. Find $3\frac{7}{8}\%$ of $108,270.00

11. Calculate a 7% tax on a sale of $45.00.

12. Calculate a 5% tax on a sale of $24.99.

13. What percent of 288 is 24?

14. What percent of $1,451.86 is $326.66?

15. What percent of $1,451.86 is $29.75?

16. What percent of 160 is 66?

Find the amount and the percent of increase or decrease in annual salary for these employees. Use a plus sign (+) to indicate increase. Use a minus sign (−) to indicate decrease.

	Employee	This Year	Last Year	Increase or Decrease Amount	Percent
17.	B. Carela	$20,798.82	$19,335.15	$_____	$_____
18.	R. Nibbs	$23,425.93	$21,616.62	$_____	$_____
19.	A. Sanudo	$25,598.85	$25,857.42	$_____	$_____
20.	D. Mantee	$29,226.54	$22,370.59	$_____	$_____

Complete Problems 21 through 28. Set the Decimal Point Selector at four. Round money amounts to the nearest cent.

Record your answers on the Answer Tab for Practice Test 3.

Find the amount of cash discount and the amount due if the cash discount is taken.

	Invoice Total	Rate of Cash Discount	Amount of Cash Discount	Amount Due
21.	$300.80	2%	$_____	$_____
22.	$426.26	2/10, n/30	$_____	$_____
23.	$501.01	5/10, n/60	$_____	$_____
24.	$999.89	3%	$_____	$_____

Find the amount of trade discount and the net price.

	List Price	Trade Discount Rate	Amount	Net Price
25.	$1,690	20%	$_____	$_____
26.	$2,584	30%	$_____	$_____
27.	$6,666	35%	$_____	$_____
28.	$7,625	25%	$_____	$_____

Complete Problems 29 through 35. Set the Decimal Point Selector at four. For Problems 29 through 31, express the percents to the nearest hundredth. Round off money amounts to the nearest cent.

Record your answers on the Answer Tab for Practice Test 3.

Find the complement of the trade discount and the net price.

	List Price	Trade Discount	Complement of Trade Discount	Net Price
29.	$0,008	25%	_____ %	$ _____
30.	$6,060	$33\frac{1}{3}$%	_____ %	$ _____
31.	$2,375	$37\frac{1}{2}$%	_____ %	$ _____

Find the net price.

	List Price	Series Trade Discount	Net Price
32.	$193.54	10%, 10%, 10%	$ _____
33.	$302.20	20%, 10%, 10%	$ _____
34.	$975.60	$12\frac{1}{2}$%, 10%, 5%	$ _____
35.	$850.00	25%, 5%, $2\frac{1}{2}$%	$ _____

Complete Problems 36 through 38. Round all money amounts to the nearest cent.

Record your answers on the Answer Tab for Practice Test 3.

For each of the problems, find the single complement of the series of discounts by using the table on this page. Then find the net price.

	List Price	Series Trade Discount	Decimal of Single Complement	Net Price
36.	$4,600.85	$7\frac{1}{2}$%, 5%, $2\frac{1}{2}$%	_____	$ _____
37.	$3,999.99	$12\frac{1}{2}$%, $7\frac{1}{2}$%, 5%	_____	$ _____
38.	$8,888.77	$12\frac{1}{2}$%, 10%	_____	$ _____

Rate	5%	$7\frac{1}{2}$%	10%	$12\frac{1}{2}$%
$2\frac{1}{2}$%	.92625	.90188	.8775	.85313
5%	.9025	.87875	.855	.83125
5%, $2\frac{1}{2}$%	.87994	.85678	.83363	.81047
5%, 5%	.85738	.83481	.81225	.78969
5%, 5%, $2\frac{1}{2}$%	.83594	.81394	.79194	.76995
$7\frac{1}{2}$%	.87875	.85563	.8325	.80938
$7\frac{1}{2}$%, $2\frac{1}{2}$%	.85678	.83423	.81169	.78914
$7\frac{1}{2}$%, 5%	.83481	.81284	.79088	.76891
10%	.855	.8235	.81	.7875

Complete Problems 39 through 50.

Round all money amounts in Problems 42 through 50 to the nearest cent.

Record your answers on the Answer Tab for Practice Test 3.

After you have completed Practice Test 3, check with your instructor about taking Test 3.

Find the single complement of each series of discounts. Set the Decimal Point Selector at five for these problems.

39. 15%, 10%, 7%

40. 20%, 8%, 7%

41. 35%, 10%, 5%

Extend the invoice below and then audit it.

TERMS: 2/10, *n*/60   **INVOICE NO. 333**

Quantity	Description	Unit Price	Extension	Audit	
18	No. 3303 pens	$ 7.50 ea.	$_____	_____	**42.**
12 bxs.	No. 607 erasers	$ 3.55/bx.	$_____	_____	**43.**
$3\frac{1}{2}$ gr.	No. 334 pencils	$10.75/gr.	$_____	_____	**44.**
2 C	No. 6171 pads	$ 4.75/C	$_____	_____	**45.**
		Total	$_____	_____	**46.**
		20% Trade Discount	$_____	_____	**47.**
		Net Price	$_____	_____	**48.**
		8% Sales Tax	$_____	_____	**49.**
		AMOUNT DUE	$_____	_____	**50.**

L E S S O N 21

Retailers buy merchandise at *cost* and resell it at a higher *selling price*. The difference between price and cost is called **markup**.

MARKUP BASED ON COST

Some merchants use their cost as the base for their markup. The cost is multiplied by the markup rate. The resulting amount is added to the cost to get the selling price.

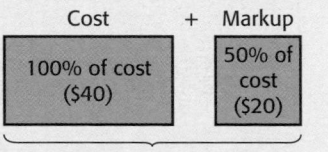

Cost	+	Markup
100% of cost ($40)		50% of cost ($20)

= Selling Price ($60)

MARKUP

Demonstration Problem

Find the markup based on cost. Then find the selling price. Cost, $40; markup rate, 50%.

1. Cost × Markup Rate = Markup Amount

2. Cost + Markup Amount = Selling Price

Enter	Press	Tape
	T	0.00 T
40	+	40.00 +
	×	40.00 ×
.50	=	.50 =
		20.00 (markup)
	+	20.00 +
	T	60.00 T (selling price)

OBJECTIVES

■ *Compute markup based on cost.*
■ *Compute markup based on selling price.*
■ *Compute markup based on selling price when only the cost and the markup rate are known.*

When the markup is based on cost, the selling price can be found in one step. Add the markup rate to 100%. Multiply the cost by the markup rate.

$$\text{Cost} \times \begin{matrix} \text{Markup Rate} \\ + 100\% \end{matrix} = \begin{matrix} \text{Selling} \\ \text{Price} \end{matrix}$$

$$\$40 \times 150\% \ (1.5) = \$60$$

Remember to estimate your answers first.

Set the Decimal Point Selector at two and the Round switch in the four/five position. For Problems A and 1 through 8, find the markup based on cost and add to find the selling price. Find the selling price in one step for Problems B and 9 through 16. Round money amounts to the nearest cent.

Record your answers on the Answer Tab for Lesson 21.

	Cost	Markup Rate	Markup	Selling Price
A.	$50.00	22%	$ 11.00	$ 61.00
1.	$46.75	40%	$	$
2.	$28.50	35%	$	$
3.	$32.75	$37\frac{1}{2}\%$	$	$
4.	$ 5.25	45%	$	$
5.	$75.00	50%	$	$
6.	$75.00	$33\frac{1}{3}\%$	$	$
7.	$12.50	$17\frac{1}{2}\%$	$	$
8.	$67.50	60%	$	$

	Cost	Markup Rate	Selling Price
B.	$ 67.50	25%	$ 84.38
9.	$ 75.15	35%	$
10.	$ 12.25	$22\frac{1}{2}\%$	$
11.	$ 43.65	45%	$
12.	$ 32.00	50%	$
13.	$124.75	$33\frac{1}{3}\%$	$
14.	$ 46.30	45%	$
15.	$ 86.90	35%	$
16.	$ 35.25	42%	$

MARKUP BASED ON SELLING PRICE

When markup is based on selling price, selling price equals 100%. To find the markup amount, multiply the markup rate by the selling price. To find the cost, subtract the markup amount from the selling price.

Notice that a 50% markup based on cost equals a $33\frac{1}{3}$% markup based on selling price.

Be sure to use the right base.

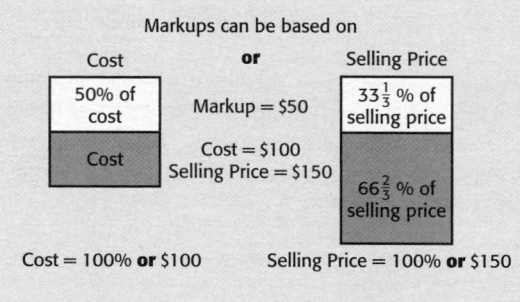

Markups can be based on

Cost	**or**	Selling Price
50% of cost	Markup = $50	$33\frac{1}{3}$ % of selling price
Cost	Cost = $100 Selling Price = $150	$66\frac{2}{3}$ % of selling price

Cost = 100% **or** $100   Selling Price = 100% **or** $150

Demonstration Problem

Find the markup and cost. Selling price, $150; markup rate based on selling price, $33\frac{1}{3}$%.

1. Selling Price × Markup Rate = Markup

2. Selling Price − Markup = Cost

Enter	Press	Tape
	T	0.00 T
150	+	150.00 +
	×	150.00 ×
.33333	=	.3333
	−	50.00 − (markup, rounds to $50)
	T	100.00 T (cost is $100)

NOTE: You can find the cost in one step if you use the *complement* of the markup rate. The **complement** of the markup rate is the markup rate subtracted from 100%. The complement of $33\frac{1}{3}$% equals $66\frac{2}{3}$%.

Selling Price	×	Markup Rate's Complement	=	Cost
$150	×	.66667	=	$100.00 (rounds to $100)

Use the complement of the markup rate to find the cost in Problems 17 through 24. Check Problem C. Set the Decimal Point Selector at two. Record your answers on the Answer Tab for Lesson 21.

	Selling Price	Markup Rate	Comple- ment	Cost
C.	$120.00	25%	75 %	$ 90
17.	$ 82.50	20%	%	$
18.	$ 92.00	30%	%	$
19.	$ 67.95	$37\frac{1}{2}$%	%	$
20.	$ 97.75	60%	%	$
21.	$137.50	33%	%	$
22.	$210.98	$42\frac{1}{2}$%	%	$
23.	$225.85	45%	%	$
24.	$165.50	27%	%	$

Use the markup rate to find the markup and subtract to find the cost in Problems 25 through 40. Check Problem D. Record your answers on the Answer Tab for Lesson 21.

	Selling Price	Markup Rate	Markup	Cost
D.	$ 99.99	$33\frac{1}{3}$%	$ 33.33	$ 66.66
25.	$ 67.25	$22\frac{1}{2}$%	$	$
26.	$ 75.75	30%	$	$
27.	$ 65.96	40%	$	$
28.	$ 46.75	$37\frac{1}{2}$%	$	$
29.	$ 88.95	34%	$	$
30.	$ 92.50	35%	$	$
31.	$240.50	$37\frac{1}{2}$%	$	$
32.	$264.25	35%	$	$
33.	$408.88	38%	$	$
34.	$256.66	40%	$	$
35.	$750.00	46%	$	$
36.	$226.00	34%	$	$
37.	$444.99	30%	$	$
38.	$139.98	45%	$	$
39.	$575.00	55%	$	$
40.	$379.98	43%	$	$

FINDING THE SELLING PRICE WHEN MARKUP IS BASED ON SELLING PRICE

Retailers who base the markup on the selling price usually know only the cost at first. The selling price can be found by dividing the cost by the complement of the markup rate.

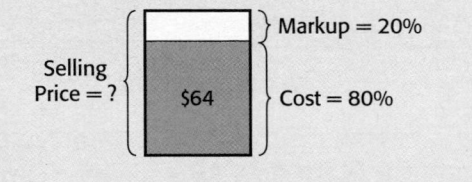

$$\text{Selling price} = \frac{\text{Cost}}{(100\% - \text{Markup Rate})}$$

$$\text{Selling price} = \frac{\$64}{80\%} = \$80$$

Demonstration Problem

Find the selling price and the markup. Cost, \$64; markup rate (based on selling price), 20%.

1. Figure the complement of the markup rate mentally (100% − 20% = 80%).

2. To find the selling price, divide the cost by the markup rate's complement.

$$\$64 \div .8 = \$80$$

3. To find the markup, subtract the cost from the selling price:

$$\$80 - \$64 = \$16$$

Enter	Press	Tape
	T	0.00 T
64	÷	64.00 ÷
.8	=	0.80 =
		80.00 (selling price)
	+	80.00 +
64	−	64.00 −
	T	16.00 T (markup amount)

Check Problem E and work Problems 41 through 53. Find the selling price and markup for each problem, using the method described above. Remember to round money amounts to the nearest cent. Record your answers on the Answer Tab for Lesson 21.

Cost	Markup Rate Based on Selling Price	Selling Price	Markup
E. $525.25	25%	$ 700.33	$ 175.08
41. $202.12	30%	$	$
42. $463.29	27%	$	$
43. $239.78	35%	$	$
44. $215.00	25%	$	$
45. $127.70	28%	$	$
46. $410.75	50%	$	$
47. $ 8.35	60%	$	$
48. $ 69.99	45%	$	$
49. $100.00	50%	$	$
50. $100.00	$33\frac{1}{3}$%	$	$
51. $ 14.75	40%	$	$
52. $ 26.00	38%	$	$

53. **Communication**   Explain how to find the markup and selling price when the markup is based on the selling price and only the cost and markup rate are known.

MARKDOWN

Markdown is a deduction from the regular selling price of an item. Markdowns are used when items are put on sale. Usually, a **markdown** is figured as a percentage of the regular selling price.

Demonstration Problem

Regular Price	×	Markdown Rate	=	Markdown
$49.95	×	25%	=	$12.49

Regular Price	−	Markdown	=	Reduced Price
$49.95	−	$12.49	=	$37.46

MARKDOWN

1. Estimate.

2. Enter the regular price as an addition.

3. To find the markdown, multiply the regular price by the markdown rate.

4. To find the reduced price, subtract the markdown from the regular price.

Estimate: $50 \times .20 = 10; 50 - 10 = 40$.

Enter	Press	Tape	
	T	0.00 T	
49.95	+	49.95 +	(regular price)
	×	49.95 ×	
.25	=	.25 =	
	−	12.49 =	(markdown)
	T	37.46 T	(reduced price)

The answer is reasonable.

For all problems in this lesson, set the Decimal Point Selector at two and the Round switch in the five/four position.

OBJECTIVES
- *Find markdowns and reduced prices.*
- *Complete Progress Test 10 within 10 minutes and without errors.*

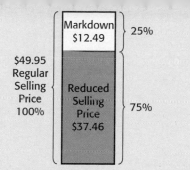

The reduced price can also be found by multiplying the regular price by the markdown's complement (100% – markdown rate). Use the regular price as the constant multiplier.

Enter	Press	Tape	
	T	0.00 T	
49.95	×	49.95 ×	
.25	=	0.25 =	
		12.49	(markdown)
.75	=	0.75 =	(complement)
		37.46	(reduced price)

Check Problem A and work Problems 1 through 15. Record your answers on the Answer Tab for Lesson 22.

	Regular Price	Markdown Rate	Markdown	Reduced Price
A.	$262.95	20%	$ 52.59	$ 210.36
1.	$171.50	25%	$	$
2.	$144.00	$22\frac{1}{2}$%	$	$
3.	$289.99	$27\frac{1}{2}$%	$	$
4.	$190.95	$12\frac{1}{2}$%	$	$
5.	$234.00	19%	$	$
6.	$396.00	$33\frac{1}{3}$%	$	$
7.	$295.00	18%	$	$
8.	$215.50	12%	$	$
9.	$155.75	16%	$	$
10.	$219.00	10%	$	$
11.	$368.99	30%	$	$
12.	$575.75	$37\frac{1}{2}$%	$	$
13.	$888.88	25%	$	$
14.	$475.99	50%	$	$
15.	$ 99.99	20%	$	$

Business Application

The ABC Discount Store is preparing for a sale and will mark down all of its prices by 25%. To the right are some of its regularly priced items. Figure the amount of markdown and the new selling price for each item listed.

Check Problem B and work Problems 16 through 29. Estimate your answers before you use your calculator. Write your answers on the Answer Tab for Lesson 22.

Regularly Priced Item	Markdown	New Selling Price
B. Ladies' sweaters, $24.00	6.00	$18.00
16. Junior sportswear, $22.00		
17. Denim shorts, $19.00		
18. Athletic shoes, $49.99		
19. Junior shorts, $25.89		
20. Athletic apparel, $29.99		
21. Men's T-shirts, $10.00		
22. Girls' tops, $11.39		
23. Toddlers' dresses, $14.99		
24. Men's denim jeans, $21.99		
25. Sunglasses, $28.00		
26. Clogs, $21.00		
27. Casual sandals, $19.99		
28. Bath towels, $7.99		
29. Girls' shorts, $15.99		

REVIEW

The problems on the right are a review of (1) mark-down and (2) markup based on selling price when the cost and rate of markup are known.

Check Problems C and D, and work Problems 30 through 42. Estimate your answers before you use your calculator.

After you complete Lesson 22, check with your instructor about taking Progress Test 10 on pages 236 and 237.

	Regular Price	Markdown Rate	Markdown	Reduced Price
C.	$171.00	20%	$34.20	$136.80
30.	$144.00	15%		
31.	$234.00	30%		
32.	$368.99	25%		
33.	$124.99	15%		
34.	$ 99.99	10%		
35.	$289.99	20%		

Mentally find the complement of the markup rate and divide the cost by the complement to get the selling price.

	Cost	Markup Rate Based on Selling Price	Selling Price
D.	$ 50.00	40%	$83.33
36.	$100.00	50%	
37.	$ 79.00	30%	
38.	$ 49.99	$33\frac{1}{3}\%$	
39.	$124.00	40%	
40.	$210.00	30%	
41.	$ 33.50	40%	

42. **Communication**   Give an example of a markdown.

MONTHLY AND SEMI-MONTHLY PAYROLLS

GROSS PAY

Most paychecks are written for amounts less than full salary. Full salary, or **gross pay**, is taxed, and most employers must collect this tax for the government. The employer may also deduct insurance payments or savings deposits, as a worker requests. Amounts subtracted from gross pay are called **deductions**. The amount of the paycheck is called **net pay**.

Net Pay = Gross Pay − Deductions

Federal income tax is deducted by an employer and sent to the Internal Revenue Service (IRS). The amount of tax paid by each worker depends on gross pay, marital status, and the number of exemptions claimed. The IRS provides income tax tables that tell how much tax to deduct.

Social security and medicare rates may change from year to year. In a recent year the social security rate was 6.2% and the medicare rate was 1.45%. In the payroll lessons, assume that these taxes are deducted from the first $65,400 of taxable wages. Medicare is deducted from all taxable wages. The social security and medicare deductions must be listed separately by the employer. The IRS provides employers with tax tables that indicate how much should be deducted for each employee.

Insurance is a benefit paid sometimes by both the worker and employer. In this lesson the insurance rate is $1\frac{1}{2}\%$ of the gross pay or earnings (.015).

Payroll Periods

A monthly payroll means that a paycheck is received 12 times a year; semimonthly, 24 times; weekly, 52 times; and biweekly, 26 times.

Remember to estimate your answers first.

Demonstration Problem

Employee's gross pay	$885.25
Federal income tax	$104.00
Social security rate	6.2%
Medicare rate	1.45%
Insurance rate	1.5%

Find the amount of social security, medicare, insurance, and net pay for the above employee.

Gross Pay	×	Soc. Sec.* Rate	=	Soc. Sec. Deduction
$885.25	×	.062	=	$54.89

Gross Pay	×	Medicare Rate	=	Medicare Deduction
$885.25	×	.0145	=	$12.84

Gross Pay	×	Insurance Rate	=	Insurance Deduction
$885.25	×	.015	=	$13.28

Federal tax (from table), $104.00

Gross Pay	−	Deductions	=	Net Pay
$885.25	−	$54.89	=	$700.24
		−12.84		
		−$13.28		
		−$104.00		

* Soc. Sec. stands for "Social Security."

To find the net pay of each employee, use a continuous operation.

1. Enter the gross pay as an addition.

2. Multiply to find the social security deduction and subtract it using the ⌷=−⌷ key.

3. Multiply to find the medicare deduction and subtract it using the ⌷=−⌷ key.

4. Multiply to find the insurance deduction and subtract it using the ⌷=−⌷ key.

5. Subtract the federal income tax to find net pay.

Enter	Press	Tape	
	T	0.00 T	
885.25	+	885.25 +	(gross pay)
	×	885.25 ×	
.062	=−	.062 =−	Estimate: 900 × .06 = 54.00
		54.89	(social security deduction)
.0145	=−	0.0145 =−	Estimate: 900 × .01 = 9.00
		12.840	(medicare deduction)
.015	=−	0.015 =−	Estimate: 900 × .02 = 18.00
		13.28	(insurance deduction)
104.00	−	104.00 −	(federal income tax)
	T	700.24 T	(net pay)

If the method using ⌷=−⌷ does not work on your calculator, use ⌷=⌷, ⌷−⌷ instead. Otherwise, find the answers in separate steps.

Business Application

This payroll register lists salary and deduction information for the pay period ending January 15, 20—. Check Problems A and B. Find the social security (soc. sec.), medicare, and insurance deductions, and net pay for each employee (Problems 1 through 18). Rates are given on page 148. Finally, find total earnings (gross pay), deductions, and net pay (Problems 19 through 24) and answer Problem 25. Record your answers on the Answer Tab for Lesson 23.

PAYROLL REGISTER
Semimonthly Period Ending January 15, 20—

Employee Data				Deductions					
Name	Marital Status	Exemp.	Gross Pay	Fed. Inc. Tax	Soc. Sec. Tax	Medicare Tax	Insur-ance	Net Pay	
K. Adams	M	4	1,229 00	90 00	76 20	17 82	18 44	1,026 54	A.
S. Barato	M	2	966 00	79 00	59 89	14 01	14 49	798 61	B.
B. Beaudin	M	1	998 00	97 00					1.
L. Carter	M	3	1,088 00	83 00					2.
F. Chung	M	2	1,088 00	97 00					3.
R. Conti	M	4	1,088 00	69 00					4.
R. Dominick	M	6	1,179 00	52 00					5.
A. Garcia	S	1	990 00	119 00					6.

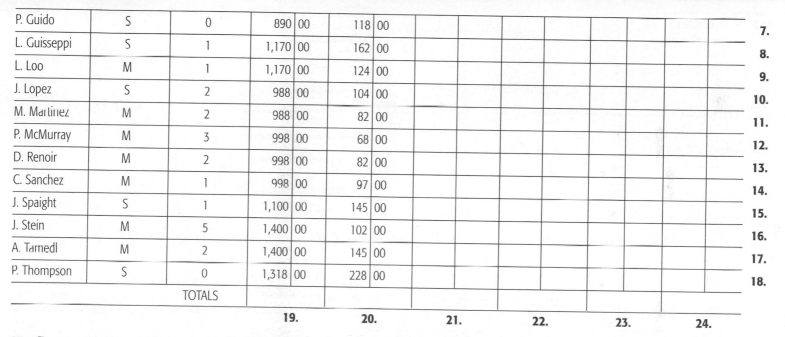

Name	Status	Allowances	Gross Pay		Deductions									
P. Guido	S	0	890	00	118	00								**7.**
L. Guisseppi	S	1	1,170	00	162	00								**8.**
L. Loo	M	1	1,170	00	124	00								**9.**
J. Lopez	S	2	988	00	104	00								**10.**
M. Martinez	M	2	988	00	82	00								**11.**
P. McMurray	M	3	998	00	68	00								**12.**
D. Renoir	M	2	998	00	82	00								**13.**
C. Sanchez	M	1	998	00	97	00								**14.**
J. Spaight	S	1	1,100	00	145	00								**15.**
J. Stein	M	5	1,400	00	102	00								**16.**
A. Tarnedl	M	2	1,400	00	145	00								**17.**
P. Thompson	S	0	1,318	00	228	00								**18.**
		TOTALS	**19.**		**20.**		**21.**		**22.**		**23.**		**24.**	

25. Communication   Explain how to find net pay.

PAYROLLS FOR HOURLY WORKERS

OBJECTIVES

- *Find regular pay, overtime rates, overtime pay, and gross pay for hourly workers.*
- *Find net pay for hourly workers.*

Workers who are paid by the hour are often paid $1\frac{1}{2}$ times their regular rate for *overtime*. **Overtime** (O.T.) hours are those worked over 40 hours per week.

Remember to estimate your answers first.

Demonstration Problem

Hours worked, 45; regular rate $9/hr

Reg. Hours	×	Reg. Rate	=	Reg. Pay
40	×	$9	=	$360

O.T. Hours	×	O.T. Rate	=	O.T. Pay
5	×	$13.50	=	$67.50
		($9 × $1\frac{1}{2}$)		

Reg. Pay	+	O.T. Pay	=	Gross Pay
$360	+	$67.50	=	$427.50

1. Find the overtime rate (regular rate × $1\frac{1}{2}$).

2. Find overtime pay (hours over 40 per week × overtime rate) and add.

3. Find regular pay (regular hours × regular rate) and add.

4. Find gross pay by totaling.

Enter	Press	Tape		Enter	Press	Tape
	T	0.00 T			+	67.50 +
9.00	×	9.00 ×		9.00	×	9.00 ×
1.5	=	1.50 =		40	=	40.00 =
		13.50 (O.T. rate)				360.00 (regular pay)
	×	13.50 ×			+	360.00 +
5	=	5.00 =			T	427.50 T (gross pay)
		67.50 (O.T. pay)				

GROSS EARNINGS

Find the gross pay for the hours worked as listed to the right. To find the overtime rate, multiply the regular rate by $1\frac{1}{2}$. If the overtime rate ends in a half cent, do not round the fraction of a cent until you have figured the overtime pay.

Check Problems A and B and complete Problems 1 through 15. Record your answers on the Answer Tab for Lesson 24.

Hours	Regular Rate	Regular Pay	Overtime Rate	Overtime Pay	Gross Pay	
45	$ 11.00	$ 440.00	$ 16.50	$ 82.50	$ 522.50	A.
$44\frac{1}{2}$	$ 9.75	$ 390.00	$ 14.625	$ 65.81	$ 455.81	B.
40	$ 9.25	$	$	$	$	1.
$42\frac{1}{4}$	$ 10.25	$	$	$	$	2.
39	$ 9.95	$	$	$	$	3.
$43\frac{1}{4}$	$ 9.75	$	$	$	$	4.
$41\frac{3}{4}$	$ 10.40	$	$	$	$	5.
$41\frac{1}{2}$	$ 9.95	$	$	$	$	6.
45	$ 10.35	$	$	$	$	7.
40	$ 9.75	$	$	$	$	8.
43	$ 10.65	$	$	$	$	9.
$42\frac{3}{4}$	$ 10.45	$	$	$	$	10.
$42\frac{1}{2}$	$ 10.00	$	$	$	$	11.
40	$ 9.90	$	$	$	$	12.
TOTALS		$ ___ 13.		$ ___ 14.	$ ___ 15.	

Business Application

After gross pay has been found, deductions are made as usual. Use the method shown in Lesson 23 to complete this payroll register. Deductions for federal income tax and union dues are shown. The social security tax is 6.2%; the medicare tax is 1.45%. Check Problems C, D, and E. Record your answers for Problems 16 through 41 on the Answer Tab for Lesson 24. Be sure that Gross Pay − Deductions = Net Pay. For the following problems, set the Decimal Point Selector at two.

PAYROLL REGISTER
For the Week Beginning January 16, 20— and Ending January 22, 20—

Name	Marital Status	Exemp.	Hours	Regular	Overtime	Gross Pay	Federal Income Tax	Social Security Tax	Medicare Tax	Union Dues	Net Pay	
	Employee Data				Gross Earnings				Deductions			
N. Balsam	M	1	48	345 00	103 50	448 50	43 00	27 81	6 50	2 25	368 94	C.
R. Benoit	M	2	$34\frac{3}{4}$	298 16		298 16	14 00	18 49	4 32	2 25	259 10	D.
G. Carino	S	1	$44\frac{1}{4}$	330 00	52 59	382 59	44 00	23 72	5 55	2 25	307 07	E.
S. Chen	M	2	36	313 20		313 20	17 00			2 25		16.
J. Cohen	M	4	$41\frac{1}{2}$	495 00	27 84	522 84	35 00			2 25		17.
G. Gomez	M	3	$39\frac{3}{4}$	298 13		298 13	7 00			2 25		18.
R. Hampton	M	4	$44\frac{1}{2}$	540 00	91 13	631 13	51 00			2 25		19.
M. Harkavy	M	3	$43\frac{1}{4}$	420 00	51 19	471 19	34 00			2 25		20.

Name	Type	No.	Hours																No.
D. Harris	S	1	$41\frac{1}{4}$	495	00	23	20	518	20	68	00					2	25		**21.**
K. Khoury	M	1	$43\frac{1}{2}$	420	00	55	13	475	13	47	00					2	25		**22.**
L. Klochkoff	M	1	$47\frac{1}{4}$	420	00	114	19	534	19	56	00					2	25		**23.**
E. Loo	M	1	40	390	00			390	00	35	00					2	25		**24.**
L. Ming	S	1	36	345	60			345	60	38	00					2	25		**25.**
J. Nguyen	M	1	$41\frac{3}{4}$	510	00	33	47	543	47	58	00					2	25		**26.**
L. Polski	M	0	$38\frac{1}{4}$	401	64			401	64	43	00					2	25		**27.**
M. Santini	M	1	$38\frac{1}{2}$	375	39			375	39	32	00					2	25		**28.**
K. Smathers	S	0	44	360	00	54	00	414	00	55	00					2	25		**29.**
J. Sprague	M	1	$46\frac{3}{4}$	480	00	121	50	601	50	67	00					2	25		**30.**
P. Velez	M	2	$34\frac{1}{2}$	362	25			362	25	24	00					2	25		**31.**
K. Wong	M	3	$45\frac{3}{4}$	420	00	90	56	510	56	40	00					2	25		**32.**
		TOTALS																	
				33.		**34.**		**35.**		**36.**		**37**		**38.**		**39.**		**40.**	

COMMISSION PAYROLL PLANS

OBJECTIVE

- *Find commission and gross pay using three commission plans: straight-commission, salary-plus commission, and salary-plus-bonus.*

A **commission** is a percentage of a sale paid to a salesperson. There are three common commission payroll plans.

STRAIGHT-COMMISSION PLAN

People who work for a percentage of their sales **only** are on a straight-commission payroll plan.

Total Sales × Rate = Commission
$2,083.50 × 25% = $520.88

Carolyn Pezzutti is paid 25% of her total sales of $2,083.50. Her commission equals her gross pay, $520.88.

Check Problem A. Then do Problems 1 through 10. Set the Decimal Point Selector at two and the round switch in the five/four position.

Remember to estimate your answers first.

Find the commission for these straight-commission employees. Record your answers on the Answer Tab for Lesson 25.

Employee	Sales	Rate	Commission	
C. Pezzutti	$2,083.50	25%	$ 520.88	A.
D. Wang	$1,953.30	25%	$_____	1.
E. Stein	$1,797.10	25%	$_____	2.
C. Nguyen	$1,787.50	30%	$_____	3.
P. Savalis	$1,858.40	30%	$_____	4.
L. Gomez	$2,015.35	25%	$_____	5.
P. Barry	$2,002.85	30%	$_____	6.
J. Gonzalez	$1,766.25	35%	$_____	7.
J. Malanga	$1,723.15	35%	$_____	8.
P. McPatrick	$1,799.90	35%	$_____	9.
M. Monte	$1,915.00	30%	$_____	10.

SALARY-PLUS-COMMISSION PLAN

Some salespeople receive a base salary plus a commission on their total sales.

Demonstration Problem

Jay Adams receives a $150 salary plus 2% of his total sales of $7,055. First find the commission. Then add the salary.

$$\text{Sales} \times \text{Rate} = \text{Commission}$$
$$\$7,055 \times 2\% = \$141.10$$

$$\text{Commission} + \frac{\text{Base}}{\text{Salary}} = \frac{\text{Gross}}{\text{Earnings}}$$
$$\$141.10 + \$150.00 = \$291.10$$

Enter	Press	Tape
	T	0.00 T
.02	×	.02 ×
7,055	=	7,055.00 =
		141.10
	+	141.10 +
150.00	+	150.00 +
	T	291.10 T

Find the commission and the gross pay of these salespeople. Check the demonstration problem and Problem B first. Record your answers on the Answer Tab for Lesson 25.

Employee	Total Sales	2% Commission	Base Salary	Gross Pay	
E. Adami	$ 6,757	$ 135.14	$350	$ 485.14	B.
G. Guadalupe	$ 7,765	$	$350	$	11.
C. Buono	$ 8,056	$	$350	$	12.
F. Cattinni	$ 9,729	$	$350	$	13.
A. Moy	$ 8,168	$	$350	$	14.
D. Ming	$10,960	$	$275	$	15.
P. Gomez	$ 9,378	$	$350	$	16.
R. Chang	$12,815	$	$400	$	17.
L. Pham	$ 9,105	$	$350	$	18.
P. Rosen	$10,880	$	$400	$	19.
J. Matsui	$ 7,995	$	$350	$	20.

SALARY-PLUS-BONUS PLAN

Some salespeople receive a base salary plus a bonus commission on all sales above a **quota,** or fixed amount.

Demonstration Problem

Tracy Hollister receives a base salary of $500 plus a 5% bonus commission on all sales above a weekly sales quota of $1,500. This week her sales totaled $2,153, which was $653 above her quota. Her gross earnings were $532.65, or $500 plus 5% of $653.

Sales	−	Quota	=	Bonus Sales
$2,153	−	$1,500	=	$653

Bonus Sales	×	Rate	=	Bonus
$653	×	5%	=	$32.65

Bonus	+	Salary	=	Gross Pay
$32.65	+	$500.00	=	$532.65

To find the gross pay using the salary-plus-bonus plan, use the continuous operation.

1. Find the bonus sales above the quota (sales −1 quota).

2. Find the commission bonus (bonus sales × commission rate).

3. Add the salary to the bonus to find gross pay.

Enter	Press	Tape	
	T	0.00 T	
2,153	+	2,153.00 +	
1,500	−	1,500.00 −	
	T	653.00 T	(bonus sales)
	×	653.00 ×	
.05	=	.05 =	
		32.65	(bonus)
	+	32.65 +	
500	+	500.00 +	(salary)
	T	532.65 T	(gross pay)

Business Application

Company managers need information to judge the performance of each salesperson and of the company as a whole. This sales salary report will show both the top salesperson of the week and the total sales above quota.

As a payroll assistant for the Mead Corporation, complete the report at the right. Find the sales above quota, the bonus commission, and the gross pay for each employee. Then find the column totals. These salespeople are paid a $500 salary plus a bonus of 5% on sales above a $2,500 quota weekly.

Check Problem C and work Problems 21 through 35. Record your answers on the Answer Tab for Lesson 25.

MEAD CORPORATION
Sales Salary Report
Week Ending September 23, 20—

Employee	Weekly Total Sales	Sales Above Quota	5% Bonus Commission	Weekly Gross Pay	
D. Gonzalez	$4,474	$ 1,974	$ 98.70	$ 598.70	C.
H. Mead	$3,922	$_____	$_____	$_____	21.
O. Wang	$3,962	$_____	$_____	$_____	22.
C. Chung	$4,210	$_____	$_____	$_____	23.
P. Garcia	$3,850	$_____	$_____	$_____	24.
A. Sanudo	$4,031	$_____	$_____	$_____	25.
N. Washington	$3,875	$_____	$_____	$_____	26.
A. Loo	$3,984	$_____	$_____	$_____	27.
B. Holly	$4,124	$_____	$_____	$_____	28.
L. Chang	$3,876	$_____	$_____	$_____	29.
K. Adam	$4,040	$_____	$_____	$_____	30.
TOTALS	$_____	$_____	$_____	$_____	
	31.	32.	33.	34.	

35. **Communication** Explain the salary-plus-bonus payroll plan.

Retail Calculations

To find the selling price on the TI BA-35 Solar calculator, press 2nd [CMR] to clear the registers. Press MODE for the profit margin mode. No display indicator should appear, which means FIN or STAT should not appear on the screen.

Enter two of the following: CST represents cost, SEL represents selling price, or 2nd [MU] represents markup rate. Enter the percent for 2nd [MU] as a whole number (50% is entered as 50). Press CPT , which is the computation key, and then press the unknown value CST , SEL , or 2nd [MU].

Find the selling price. Cost, $40; markup rate, 50% (demonstration problem, page 138). Remember to press 2nd [CMR] MODE first to clear the registers and to select the profit margin mode with no display. Then enter the sequence.

40 CST 50 2nd [MU] CPT SEL = 60

The selling price is $60.

Write your answers on a separate sheet of paper.

Find the selling price when the markup is based on cost.

	Cost	Markup Rate
1.	$75.00	$33\frac{1}{3}\%$
2.	$67.50	35%
3.	$37.00	40%
4.	$87.50	42%

Find the cost when the markup is based on selling price.

	Selling Price	Markup Rate
5.	$95.00	40%
6.	$48.75	$37\frac{1}{2}$%
7.	$125.00	35%
8.	$75.00	38%

Find the reduced price when the markdown is based on the regular price.

	Regular Price	Markdown Rate
9.	$24.95	10%
10.	$36.50	50%
11.	$45.00	$33\frac{1}{3}$%
12.	$98.25	20%

To find the markup and cost when the markup is based on the selling price, multiply the selling price times the markup rate. Subtract the markup from the selling price to find the cost.

Selling price $150; markup rate based on selling price, $33\frac{1}{3}$% (demonstration problem, page 140).

150 STO × 33 . 333 % = 49.95 +/− SUM RCL 2nd [MEM] =
100.05

The markup rounds from $49.95 to $50.00. The cost rounds from $100.05 to $100.00.

To find the markdown amount and the reduced price, multiply the regular price by the markdown rate. Subtract the markdown amount from the regular price.

Regular price $49.95; markdown rate is 25% (demonstration problem, page 144).

49.95 STO × 25 % = 12.4875 +/− SUM RCL 2nd [MEM] − 37.4625

The markdown amount rounds from $12.4875 to $12.49 and the reduced price rounds from $37.4625 to $32.46.

Problems 1 through 14 are a review of markup and markdown.

Set the Decimal Point Selector at two and the Round switch in the five/four position. Remember to round money amounts to the nearest cent.

Record your answers on the Answer Tab for Practice Test 4.

In Problems 1 through 4, find the markup and the selling price.

	Cost	Markup Rate Based on Cost	Markup	Selling Price
1.	$ 660	25%	$_____	$_____
2.	$1,390	30%	$_____	$_____
3.	$1,760	40%	$_____	$_____
4.	$1,400	55%	$_____	$_____

In Problems 5 through 8, find the markup and the cost.

	Selling Price	Markup Rate Based on Selling Price	Markup	Cost
5.	$ 800	20%	$_____	$_____
6.	$1,650	33%	$_____	$_____
7.	$2,130	30%	$_____	$_____
8.	$4,440	40%	$_____	$_____

Complete Problems 9 through 14. Round money amounts to the nearest cent.

Record your answers on the Answer Tab for Practice Test 4.

In Problems 9 through 11, find the selling price and the markup.

	Cost	Markup Rate Based on Selling Price	Selling Price	Markup
9.	$ 45.25	22%	$_____	$_____
10.	$ 93.00	30%	$_____	$_____
11.	$128.00	45%	$_____	$_____

In Problems 12 through 14, find the markdown and the reduced selling price.

	Regular Selling Price	Markdown Rate	Markdown	Reduced Selling Price
12.	$ 41.90	33%	$_____	$_____
13.	$ 48.00	70%	$_____	$_____
14.	$224.50	55%	$_____	$_____

Semimonthly payrolls, weekly payrolls, and commission payroll plans are reviewed in Problems 15 through 30.

Record your answers on the Answer Tab for Practice Test 4.

Find the social security and medicare taxes and the net pay for these employees.

Employee Number	Gross Pay	Soc. Sec. Tax (6.2%) Deduction	Medicare Tax (1.45%)	Fed. Inc. Tax	Net Pay
15. 110-32-0456	$945.07	$_____	$_____	$76.00	$_____
16. 111-33-0822	$676.33	$_____	$_____	$64.00	$_____
17. 113-44-0666	$848.20	$_____	$_____	$61.00	$_____

Find the weekly net pay of each of the following employees who receive $1\frac{1}{2}$ times their regular rate for overtime hours over 40 hours per week.

Employee Number	Hourly Rate	Weekly Total Hours	Weekly Total Deductions	Weekly Net Pay
18. 111-66-0222	$8.00	45	$63.75	$_____
19. 114-88-3216	$9.50	40	$58.25	$_____
20. 119-33-0214	$8.90	50	$70.22	$_____

Record your answers on the Answer Tab for Practice Test 4.

After you have completed Practice Test 4, check with your instructor about taking Test 4.

In Problems 21 through 26, find the gross pay of each employee if each had total sales of $1,000 and was paid a base salary plus commission.

Employee	Rate	Commission Amount	Base Salary	Gross Pay
21. D. Jerri	35%	$_____	$125	$_____
22. S. Toy	30%	$_____	$150	$_____
23. E. Tamedal	30%	$_____	$175	$_____
24. F. Vachino	35%	$_____	$150	$_____
25. R. McCauley	25%	$_____	$250	$_____
26. S. Lynch	33%	$_____	$200	$_____

In Problems 27 through 30, find the gross pay of each employee if each is paid a base salary plus a commission for sales above a quota.

Employee	Quota	Sales	10% Commission	Base Salary	Gross Pay
27. P. Paoli	$ 500	$2,800	$_____	$200	$_____
28. C. Mirlz	$ 750	$2,500	$_____	$250	$_____
29. S. Gradey	$ 400	$3,984	$_____	$200	$_____
30. B. Plainaski	$1,000	$3,075	$_____	$175	$_____

INVESTMENTS IN STOCKS

OBJECTIVES

- *Define corporate invest-ment, shares of stock, shareholders or stock-holders, dividends,* Wall Street Journal, *and New York Stock Exchange.*
- *Read and interpret the daily stock table transac-tions for the New York Stock Exchange.*

This unit will concentrate on investments in shares of stock, which represent ownership in a *corporation*. Those who own stocks are called **shareholders** or **stockholders**.

An **investment** is the process of putting money into a business, real estate, stocks, bonds, etc., for the purpose of making a profit or obtaining income.

READING THE STOCK TABLES IN THE DAILY PAPERS

On the right side of the next page is a section of a stock table taken from *The Wall Street Journal*, a daily financial newspaper. An explanation follows for the headings of the transactions, as well as the notations to the left of the stock names.

52 Weeks Hi Lo reports the highest and lowest prices for the past 52 weeks.

Stock is the abbreviated name of the stock.

Sym is the symbol used to list the stock on the ticker tape that gives the latest price and the size of every stock transaction. Today this "ticker tape" is an electronic display that lists the stock symbols and corresponding prices on a *Telerate* screen. The daily ticker tape can be seen at the bottom of the television screen on CNBC and CNN, or you can obtain it from on-line providers such as Quotran.

A **corporation** is a business unit that is a legal entity, chartered by a state government to act as an individual; that is, it can buy, sell, and own property; it can make contracts and pay taxes; it can sue and be sued. It can do legally whatever an individual can do.

Stocks are traded (bought and sold) on various stock exchanges. The three largest stock exchanges are the New York Stock Exchange; NASDAQ (National Association of Securities Dealers), selling *over the counter;* and the American Stock Exchange.

52 Weeks Hi	Lo	Stock	Sym	Div	Yld %	PE	Vol 100s	Hi	Lo	Close	Net Chg
59 1/4	51 3/8	Genentech	GNE	...	...	65	862	58 7/8	58 1/2	58 5/8	± 1/8
23 5/8	20	♣GenAmInv	GAM	2.96e	13.3	...	168	22 3/8	22 1/4	22 1/4	± 1/8
R▼ 22 1/8	20 5/8	GenICbl	GCN	...	...	...	1973	20 7/8	20 3/8	20 3/4	± 1/4
▲ 24 3/8	16 5/8	GenIChemGp	GCG	.20	.8	12	154	25 1/4	24	25	+ 1
n 29 7/8	20	GenCigar	MPP	...	...	...	476	29	28 5/8	29	...
18	6 1/8	GenData	GDC	...	...	dd	420	9 1/4	9	9 1/8	+ 1/8
75 1/2	57 1/2	GenDynam	GD	1.64	2.2	17	1700	70 7/8	73 1/4	73 5/8	+ 1/8
s 63 1/4	38 7/8	GenElec	GE	1.04	1.7	27	39660	61 1/4	60 1/2	61	+ 1/8

Div is an estimate of the annual dividend per share in dollars and cents. Note that Genentech, the first stock listed, does not pay a dividend. Note that the estimated dividend for GenElec (General Electric) is $1.04 per share. A stockholder who owns 100 shares of GenElec stock will receive an annual dividend of $104.00 (100 × $1.04). Dividends change from year to year on any given stock.

Yld % means the percent yield of the dividend, which is what percent the dividend is of the current price (the dividend divided by the current price).

PE is the price/earnings ratio, that shows the relationship between the stock's price and the earnings for the past year. The stock tables do not give the earnings, so the P/E cannot be figured from the information in the table. The P/E is figured by dividing the current stock price by the earnings per share. A P/E ratio of 65, as shown in the first line of the table, means that the stock price is 65 times the annual earnings per share.

Vol 100s refers to the number of shares traded that day. The number listed must be multiplied by 100 to find the actual volume. The volume for Genentech is 86,200 (862 × 100) shares traded.

The next three columns, **Hi, Lo, Close**, give the highest, lowest, and closing prices, respectively, for the stock traded the previous day.

The last column, **Net Chg**, compares the closing price listed with the previous closing price. The net change for Genentech is minus $\frac{1}{8}$ of a dollar, or 12.5 cents. The net change is expressed as a plus or minus. If there is no change, three dots (…) are recorded.

The symbols to the left of the **Hi** column stand for the following: the down arrow means the price hit a new 52-week low; the up arrow indicates the price hit a new 52-week high; **n** means a newly issued stock in the past 52 weeks; **s** stands for a stock split or stock dividend in the past 52 weeks. The symbol to the left of the stock GenAmInv is a free reader service available from *The Wall Street Journal*.

Answer questions 1 through 13 at the right and on the following page. Record your answers on the Answer Tab for Lesson 26.

1. **Communication**   Define a corporation.

2. **Communication**   What is an investment?

3. **Communication**   Define shares of stock.

4. **Communication**   Who are shareholders?

5. **Communication**   What is the New York Stock Exchange?

52 Weeks Hi	Lo	Stock	Sym	Div	Yld %	PE	Vol 100s	Hi	Lo	Close	Net Chg
57	46⅛	♣Penney JC	JCP	2.08	4.2	21	4512	49½	48⅝	49	+ ¼
48⅛	37⅝	♣PennEntr	PNT	2.32f	5.1	50	123	45⅞	45¼	45¾	+ ⅛
80¾	56	PennP&L pfB		4.50	5.7	...	z1120	79⅝	79⅜	79⅜	...
63½	36⅞	Pennzoil	PZL	1.00	1.8	19	2365	56⅛	55⅜	56	± ¼
26¾	17⅝	PensnProvd	PVD	1.22e	5.6	...	21	21⅞	21¾	21⅞	± ⅛
32¼	24	Pentair	PNR	.54f	1.8	17	442	31	30½	30¾	+ ¼
37⅜	29⅝	♣PeopEngy	PGL	1.88f	5.3	12	440	35¼	34⅝	35¼	+ ½
38¼	27⅞	♣PepBoys	PBY	.21	.6	21	2078	34¼	33½	33½	± ⅝
10⅝	3⅞	PepsiPR B	PPO		...	...	183	4½	4⅜	4½	+ ¼
s 35⅞	28	PepsiCo	PEP	.46	1.4	44	28172	32⅛	31¾	32	+ ¼
77⅛	44¼	PerkElmer	PKN	.68	.9	41	2554	73	72⅛	72⅜	± ⅝
14⅞	11¾	PerkFamR	PFR	1.30	9.1	11	140	14½	14	14¼	...
4⅞	3⅛	PermRltyTr	PRT	.50e	11.4	...	20	4½	4⅜	4⅜	...
29⅛	17½	PrsnlGpAm	PGA		...	23	124	25⅝	25¼	25⅝	+ ⅛
16⅜	11¾	♣PetroCnda g	PCZ	.20	...	...	28	14¾	14⅝	14⅝	± ⅛
37¼	28⅞	PeteRes	PEO	2.14e	6.2	...	155	34⅜	34⅛	34¼	...
n 21¼	11½	PfeifferVac	PV		...	...	146	21	19⅞	21	+ ¾
99¾	61½	♣Pfizer	PFE	1.36f	1.4	32	16894	97⅛	95¼	96⅞	+ 2¾
8¾	3⅛	PharmRes	PRX		...	dd	204	3⅜	3¼	3¼	± ⅛
44⅝	34⅛	PharmUpjhn	PNU	1.00	2.7	37	14741	40	39¼	40	+ ⅞
77⅝	54⅝	PhelpsD	PD	2.00	2.7	11	4157	75¼	73⅛	74¾	+ 1¾
s 20⅝	14½	PhilaSub	PSC	.81	4.1	18	444	20¼	19⅞	20	+ ⅛
18⅜	6⅛	♣PhilipEnvr g	PEV		...	...	5432	16⅞	16½	16¾	...
▲137⅞	85⅝	PhilipMor	MO	4.80	3.5	18	28172	139	136¼	138¾	+ 2¾
65¾	50	PhilLongD	PHI		...	...	1573	61½	61⅛	61½	± ⅛
59½	50	PhilLongD pf		4.12	7.3	...	1171	56⅝	56¼	56½	+ ⅜
48⅞	28¾	PhilipsNV	PHG	.99e	2.1	38	2956	46⅞	46¼	46⅞	± ¼
26¾	24⅞	PhilipsGas pfA		2.33	9.0	...	31	26⅛	26	26	± ⅛
46⅞	36¼	PhillipsPete	P	1.28	3.0	9	13532	42⅛	41½	42	...
n 26¼	23	PhilpsCap TOPrS		2.06	8.0	...	58	25⅝	25½	25⅝	...
15⅛	10¼	PhillipsVanH	PVH	.15	1.0	26	659	14⅝	14	14⅜	+ ⅜

Refer to the stock table at left to answer the following questions.

6. What is the stock symbol for JCPenney?

7. What was the closing price of PepsiCo?

8. What was the net change for Pfizer from the previous day?

9. What is the P/E ratio for JCPenney?

10. What were the highest and lowest prices in the past 52 weeks for JCPenney?

11. What was the annual dividend per share for JCPenney stock?

12. What is the dividend yield on JCPenney stock?

13. What was the volume of shares traded for PepBoys stock?

INVESTMENTS IN BONDS

OBJECTIVES

- *Define bonds.*
- *Name three types of bonds.*
- *Define the different terms of bonds and the par value of a bond.*
- *Explain fixed-income securities.*

Bonds, which are fixed-income securities, are loans that investors make to corporations and governments. The investors earn interest and the corporation or government gets the cash they need for expansion, operations, or governmental projects.

Because bonds pay a set amount of interest on a regular basis, they are called **fixed-income securities.** In contrast, stocks pay dividends as set by a board of directors, and the amounts of dividends can change periodically.

There are three types of bonds—*corporate bonds; U.S. government bonds,* which include *U.S. Treasury bills, notes and bonds;* and *municipal bonds.* The **term,** or life, of a bond is fixed at the time it is issued. **Short-term bonds,** such as treasury bills, are for a year or less; **intermediate-term bonds,** including treasury notes, usually run from two to ten years; and **long-term bonds** are for 30 years or more.

When bonds are issued, they are usually sold at **par** or face value in units of $1,000. If bonds are sold at a **discount,** it means they are sold at less than par. If they are sold at a **premium,** they are sold above par. A $1,000 bond sold for $990 is sold at a discount for a price of 99 (.99 × $1,000 = $990). A price of 100 is *par.* A $1,000 bond sold at a premium of 101 will sell for $1,010 (1.01 × $1,000 = $1,010). Corporate bond prices are given in increments of points and eight fractions of a point, with a base of $1,000 as par. The value of a point is $10, so a price of 100 equals $1,000 (100 × 10 = $1,000). Each fraction ($\frac{1}{8}$ point) is equal to $1.25.

Read the closing price of each of the corporate bonds in the list below, beginning with AMR8.10s98 (AMR 8.1% bond due in 1998). The price of $101\frac{5}{8}$ equals $1,016.25 (101 = $1,010 and $\frac{5}{8}$ = $6.25). The list continues:

$$110\frac{7}{8} \; = \; \$1,108.75$$

$$95\frac{1}{8} \; = \; 951.25$$

$$99\frac{7}{8} \; = \; 998.75$$

$$100\frac{3}{4} \; = \; 1,007.50$$

$$103\frac{5}{8} \; = \; 1,036.25$$

$$105\frac{7}{8} \; = \; 1,058.75$$

$$102\frac{5}{8} \; = \; 1,026.25$$

$$105 \; = \; 1,050.00$$

$$109 \; = \; 1,090.00$$

CORPORATE BOND TABLE

Bonds	Cur Yld	Vol	Close	Net Chg
AMR 8.10s98	8.0	24	$101\frac{5}{8}$	$-\frac{1}{8}$
AMR 9s16	8.1	6	$110\frac{7}{8}$	$+\frac{7}{8}$
ATT $5\frac{1}{8}$01	5.4	88	$95\frac{1}{8}$	$+\frac{1}{8}$
ATT $6\frac{3}{4}$04	6.8	20	$99\frac{7}{8}$	$+\frac{1}{8}$
ATT 7s05	6.9	51	$100\frac{3}{4}$	$-\frac{1}{4}$
ATT $7\frac{1}{2}$06	7.2	20	$103\frac{5}{8}$	$-1\frac{1}{4}$
ATT $7\frac{3}{4}$07	7.3	1	$105\frac{7}{8}$	$+1\frac{1}{8}$
ATT $8\frac{1}{8}$22	7.9	175	$102\frac{5}{8}$	$-\frac{1}{8}$
ATT 8.35s25	8.0	1	105	$+\frac{1}{2}$
Aamos $10\frac{1}{2}$02	9.6	15	109	$+$ 4

Complete Problems 1 through 20. Write your answers on the Answer Tab for Lesson 27.

Convert the following corporation bond prices to the equivalent dollar and cents price per $1,000 bond.

Remember to estimate your answers. Estimate $1,000 \times 87\frac{3}{8}$ as $1,000 \times .87 -$ $870.00. Check to see if your answer is reasonable.

1. $98\frac{1}{8}$ 11. $95\frac{3}{8}$

2. 111   12. $97\frac{5}{8}$

3. $105\frac{3}{8}$ 13. $99\frac{7}{8}$

4. 100   14. $101\frac{1}{4}$

5. $97\frac{1}{4}$ 15. $100\frac{1}{2}$

6. 102   16. $101\frac{3}{4}$

7. $65\frac{1}{8}$ 17. 105

8. 108   18. $104\frac{1}{2}$

9. $103\frac{1}{4}$ 19. $97\frac{7}{8}$

10. $100\frac{3}{4}$ 20. 99

21. **Communication**   Name three types of bonds that are issued.

YIELDS ON INVESTMENTS

OBJECTIVES

- *Define yield on investments.*
- *Read the dividend yields in stock tables.*
- *Read the yields on corporate bonds in newspaper tables.*

DIVIDEND YIELDS

Investors want to know what the annual rate of return, or yield, is on their investment. Yields on investments are expressed in percents.

Refer to the stock table on page 169 and read the amounts earned on various stocks. The dividend yields range from .6% on PepBoys stock to 11.4% on PermRltyTr stock. That yield changes as the price of the stock changes. Remember that the yield listed for any stock is what percent the dividend is of the *current* price (the dividend divided by the current price).

YIELDS ON STOCK INVESTMENTS

If an investor wants to know the yield on his or her investment in the stock market, then he or she must divide the dividend by the cost per share. If the annual dividend per share of GenElec stock is $1.04 (see the table on page 167), the yield is 1.7% on $61.00 per share. However, the yield on the same stock bought at a cost of $39.00 per share would be 2.7%.

YIELDS ON BOND INVESTMENTS

Refer to the corporate bond table on page 171. The rate of interest that each corporate bond pays is the number to the right of the name of the bond. For example, the first two bonds listed pay annual interest of 8.10% and 9%, respectively. The dates following the rate are the maturity dates of 1998 and 2016, respectively. The corresponding current yields are 8% and 8.1% because both bonds are currently selling at a premium above 100.

Answer Problems 1 through 20 at the right and record your answers on the Answer Tab for Lesson 28.

Use the corporate bond table on page 171. Record the interest rates and maturity dates for all the ATT bonds.

	Rate	Maturity			Rate	Maturity
1.	____%	_____		**5.**	____%	_____
2.	____%	_____		**6.**	____%	_____
3.	____%	_____		**7.**	____%	_____
4.	____%	_____				

Use the table on page 169. Find the yield (rounded to the nearest tenth of a percent) on the following shares of stock based on the cost given below.

	Stock	Cost per Share	Yield			Stock	Cost per Share	Yield
8.	PenneyJC	$47.00	____%		**14.**	PharmUpjhn	$34.50	____%
9.	PeopEngy	30.00	____%		**15.**	PhelpsD	54.75	____%
10.	Pennzoil	37.00	____%		**16.**	PhilipMor	86.00	____%
11.	PepBoys	28.00	____%		**17.**	PhilpsGas	25.00	____%
12.	PepsiCo	28.00	____%		**18.**	PhilpsCap	23.25	____%
13.	PeteRes	29.00	____%		**19.**	PhillipsVanH	11.00	____%

20. Communication How does an investor find the yield on the cost of his or her investment in stocks?

LESSON 29

SELLING PRICE OF STOCKS

GOING PUBLIC

Going public means that a company issues stock for the first time, making it possible for investors to buy the stock. Going public also means that the company is making an initial public offering, referred to as an **IPO**.

OBJECTIVES

- *Define IPO, SEC, investment bankers, going public, and prospectus.*
- *Read stock prices from stock tables.*
- *Convert fractions of eighths and sixteenths to cents equivalents.*

INVESTMENT BANKERS

When a company goes public, it goes to *investment bankers,* who agree to **underwrite** the stock offering. This means that they agree to buy all the public shares at a set price and resell them to the public at a higher price for a profit. The underwriters prepare a **prospectus,** a legal document that must be available to any investor.

The prospectus details the financial history of the company, its products or services, and the experience and background of the management team. The underwriters price the issue the day before the sale, establishing the price they will pay the company for each share.

When the stock begins to trade, the price is set by *stockbrokers,* who buy and sell the stock. Stockbrokers pass an exam on securities law and are registered with the **Securities and Exchange Commission (SEC),** which regulates the securities industry.

STOCK PRICES

From the creation of the New York Stock Exchange in 1792 until mid-1997, stock prices were offered in increments of one-eighth of one dollar, or 12.5 cents. Beginning in late June 1997, this increment was changed to one-sixteenth of a dollar, or 6.25 cents. The NASDAQ Stock Market and the American Stock Exchange began trading in the smaller increments several weeks earlier. The trading in smaller increments is an interim step to trading in decimals.

CENTS EQUIVALENTS OF EIGHTHS AND SIXTEENTHS

It is important to know the cents equivalents of the eighth and sixteenth fractions to read stock quotations correctly.

$\frac{1}{16}$ = 6.25 cents	$\frac{2}{16}$ or $\frac{1}{8}$ = 12.5 cents
$\frac{3}{16}$ = 18.75 cents	$\frac{4}{16}$ or $\frac{1}{4}$ = 25.0 cents
$\frac{5}{16}$ = 31.25 cents	$\frac{6}{16}$ or $\frac{3}{8}$ = 37.5 cents
$\frac{7}{16}$ = 43.75 cents	$\frac{8}{16}$ or $\frac{1}{2}$ = 50.0 cents
$\frac{9}{16}$ = 56.25 cents	$\frac{10}{16}$ or $\frac{5}{8}$ = 62.5 cents
$\frac{11}{16}$ = 68.75 cents	$\frac{12}{16}$ or $\frac{3}{4}$ = 75.0 cents
$\frac{13}{16}$ = 81.25 cents	$\frac{14}{16}$ or $\frac{7}{8}$ = 87.5 cents
$\frac{15}{16}$ = 93.75 cents	

To convert the cents to a part of a dollar, move the decimal point two places to the left and add the $ sign, for example, 6.25 cents = $.0625.

Practice reading the closing prices of some of the stocks listed at the right. Round the prices to the nearest cent. Note that some of the prices are listed in increments of sixteenths.

Read the dollar and cents prices (rounded to the nearest cent) of some stocks listed in the table below:

52 Weeks Hi	52 Weeks Lo	Stock	Sym	Div	Yld %	PE	Vol 100s	Hi	Lo	Close	Net Chg
21 1/4	12 3/4	BedfdPrpty	BED	1.08f	5.7	16	1092	19	18 7/8	18 15/16	+ 3/16
n 11 1/2	10 3/4	BeijngYan	BYH		...	...	3367	11	10 3/4	11	...
37 1/4	18 1/8	BelcoOG	BOG		...	16	324	22 1/2	21 5/8	21 5/8	− 1
39 7/8	24 3/4	♣Belden	BWC	.20	.6	16	3751	34 7/8	33 3/4	33 15/16	− 11/16
34 7/8	19 1/8	BellHowell	BHW		...	21	261	29 1/2	28 3/4	29	− 3/8
78 1/4	55 1/8	♣BellAtlantic	BEL	2.96f	4.0	18	7798	75 9/16	73	73 3/4	− 1 1/4
s 20	12 1/2	♣Bellindus	BI		...	11	163	16 1/8	15 3/4	15 3/4	− 7/16
48 5/8	35 1/4	BellSouth	BLS	1.44	3.2	17	15173	45 9/16	44 1/8	44 3/8	− 1 3/16
43	33 1/4	Belo AH A	BLC	.44	1.1	19	880	42 3/8	41 1/4	41 3/8	− 7/8
▲ 43 3/4	28 7/8	♣Bemis	BMS	.80	1.9	23	547	43 13/16	42 1/2	42 3/4	− 1
39 1/8	24 1/4	BenchmkElec	BHE		...	19	207	38 7/8	37 7/8	38 3/4	+ 1/2
76	50 7/8	Beneficial	BNL	2.08	3.0	14	813	71 1/2	70	70 1/8	− 7/8
33	20 5/8	Benetton	BNG	.58r	1.8	...	14	32 7/8	32 3/8	32 7/8	− 1/8
25 1/4	18 1/4	Berlitz	BTZ		...	60	14	24 3/4	24 5/8	24 3/4	+ 1/8
16 3/4	10 3/8	BerryPete	BRY	.40	2.6	18	317	15 5/8	15 1/16	15 3/8	+ 1/2
x 39 1/8	22	BestBuyCap pf		3.25	9.6	...	278	34	33 3/8	33 3/4	+ 1/8
23 3/4	7 7/8	BestBuy	BBY		...	dd	15157	15	14 1/8	14 15/16	+ 9/16
12	7 5/8	BethSteel	BS		...	dd	14936	10 3/4	10 7/16	10 11/16	+ 3/16
14 7/8	13 1/2	BlkrkCal2008	BFC	.77	5.3	...	106	14 7/16	14 3/8	14 7/16	+ 1/16
15 1/2	13 3/4	BlkrkFla2008	BRF	.86	5.6	...	101	15 1/4	15 1/8	15 1/4	...
6 3/4	5 7/8	BlkrkIncTr	BKT	.56	8.4	...	1868	6 11/16	6 5/8	6 11/16	...
10 5/8	9 7/8	BlkrkMuni	BMT	.62	5.9	...	229	10 1/2	10 7/16	10 1/2	+ 1/16
14 7/8	13 7/8	BlkrkMuni2008	BRM	.80a	5.4	...	338	14 13/16	14 5/8	14 3/4	+ 1/8
13 1/4	11 3/4	BlkrkInvQty	BKN	.79a	6.0	...	195	13 1/8	13 1/16	13 1/16	− 1/16
8 1/8	7 1/2	BlkrIdnv	BQT	.58	7.3	...	379	8	7 15/16	7 15/16	− 1/16
10 7/8	10	BlkrkMuniTr	BMN	.62	5.8	...	638	10 11/16	10 5/8	10 5/8	...
15 1/4	13 7/8	BlkrkNY2008	BLN	.86a	5.7	...	124	15 1/8	15 1/8	15 1/8	− 1/8
n 10 1/2	9 1/4	BlkrkNoAm	BNA	.84	8.2	...	868	10 1/4	10 3/16	10 1/4	+ 1/16

BedfdPrpty	$18\frac{15}{16}$	$= \$18.94$
BelcoOG	$21\frac{5}{8}$	$= 21.63$
Belden	$33\frac{15}{16}$	$= 33.94$
BellAtlantic	$73\frac{3}{4}$	$= 73.75$
Bell South	$44\frac{3}{8}$	$= 44.38$
BethSteel	$10\frac{11}{16}$	$= 10.69$

Complete Problems 1 through 21 and write your answers on the Answer Tab for Lesson 29. Before you work Problems 1 through 20, check Problems A and B. Find the total cost of the number of shares given in each of the problems (1 through 20). Do not round the per-share cost, but round your total cost to the nearest cent.

Remember to estimate your answers.

Estimate Problem A as 50 × 19 = $950.00.
Compared to the estimate, the answer is reasonable.

	Shares	Cost per share	Total		Shares	Cost per share	Total
A.	50	$18\frac{15}{16}$	$ 946.88	**B.**	100	$10\frac{11}{16}$	$1,068.75
1.	50	$14\frac{7}{16}$	_____	**11.**	100	$7\frac{11}{16}$	_____
2.	25	$13\frac{1}{16}$	_____	**12.**	50	$26\frac{7}{8}$	_____
3.	100	$6\frac{11}{16}$	_____	**13.**	45	$16\frac{3}{8}$	_____
4.	23	$10\frac{5}{8}$	_____	**14.**	65	$16\frac{3}{16}$	_____
5.	22	$25\frac{13}{16}$	_____	**15.**	50	$33\frac{9}{16}$	_____
6.	20	$25\frac{3}{16}$	_____	**16.**	100	$12\frac{3}{16}$	_____
7.	12	$60\frac{7}{16}$	_____	**17.**	75	$15\frac{5}{16}$	_____
8.	14	$58\frac{15}{16}$	_____	**18.**	100	$31\frac{3}{4}$	_____
9.	25	$32\frac{7}{16}$	_____	**19.**	50	$24\frac{1}{4}$	_____
10.	50	$25\frac{5}{16}$	_____	**20.**	33	$27\frac{13}{16}$	_____

21. Communication What is the role of the investment banker in an initial public offering of stock?

22. Communication Define the role of the stockbroker in an initial public offering (IPO).

23. Communication Explain the purpose of the prospectus.

Business Calculator Applications 5 covers U.S. government securities. U.S. Treasury notes and bonds are priced differently than stocks and corporation bonds. U.S. Treasury notes and bonds are quoted in 32nds. A price of 100:01 means $100:\frac{1}{32}$. Each $\frac{1}{32}$ is equal to 31.25 cents. At the right is a table of Treasury notes and bonds as listed in the financial pages. The column headings are: **Rate,** the annual rate of interest paid on the principal amount; **Maturity Mo/Yr,** the month and year of maturity; **Bid Asked,** the highest price offered by the buyer and the lowest priced asked by the seller, respectively; **Chg,** the change in bid prices from the previous day; and **Ask Yld,** the yield on the selling price to maturity.

Prices of Treasury Bonds and Notes

To read the prices of Treasury bonds and notes, you will have to complete a schedule of decimal values of 32nds. The values for $\frac{1}{32}$ to $\frac{4}{32}$ are shown below.

$$\frac{1}{32} = 31.25 \text{ cents}$$
$$\frac{2}{32} = 62.5 \text{ cents}$$
$$\frac{3}{32} = 93.75 \text{ cents}$$
$$\frac{4}{32} = \$1.25$$

Since each $\frac{1}{32}$ equals 31.25 cents, multiply 31.25 times every number between 5 and 31 to find the decimal values of $\frac{1}{32}$ to $\frac{31}{32}$.

Treasury Bonds and Notes

Treasury bond, note, and bill quotes are as of mid-afternoon. Colons in bond and note bid-and-asked quotes represent 32nds; 101:01 means 101 1/32. Net changes in 32nds.

Govt. Bonds and Notes

Rate	Maturity Mo/Yr	Bid	Asked	Chg.	Ask Yld.	Rate	Maturity Mo/Yr	Bid	Asked	Chg.	Ask Yld.
8½	Jul 97n	100:01	100:03	−1	5.45	6⅜	Jan 00n	100:20	100:22	+1	6.08
5½	Jul 97n	99:31	100:01	...	4.98	7¾	Jan 00n	103:24	103:26	+1	6.12
5⅞	Jul 97n	100:00	100:02	...	4.94	5⅞	Feb 00n	99:11	99:13	+1	6.12
6½	Aug 97n	100:03	100:05	+1	5.05	8½	Feb 00n	105:18	105:20	...	6.14
8⅝	Aug 97n	100:10	100:12	−1	5.28	7⅛	Feb 00n	102:10	102:12	+1	6.14
5⅝	Aug 97n	99:31	100:01	...	5.33	6⅞	Mar 00n	101:24	101:26	+1	6.14
6	Aug 97n	100:01	100:03	...	5.30	5½	Apr 00n	98:10	98:12	+1	6.14
5½	Sep 97n	99:31	100:01	...	5.29	6¼	Apr 00n	101:14	101:16	+1	6.16
5¾	Sep 97n	100:01	100:01	+1	5.28	6⅜	May 00n	100:17	100:18	+1	6.15
8¾	Oct 97n	100:28	100:30	+1	5.30	6⅞	May 00n	107:02	107:04	+1	6.12
5⅝	Oct 97n	100:00	100:02	+1	5.38	6¼	May 00n	100:06	100:08	+1	6.15
5¾	Oct 97n	100:01	100:03	+1	5.40	6⅛	Jun 00n	99:06	99:08	+1	6.15
7⅞	Nov 97n	100:19	100:21	+1	5.50	6⅛	Jul 00n	99:26	99:28	+2	6.17
8⅞	Nov 97n	101:04	101:06	+1	5.51	8¾	Aug 00n	107:04	107:06	+2	6.18
5⅜	Nov 97n	99:29	99:31	+2	5.43	6¼	Aug 00n	100:03	100:05	+1	6.19
6	Nov 97n	100:05	100:07	+1	5.42	6⅛	Sep 00n	99:23	99:25	+2	6.20
5¼	Dec 97n	99:27	99:29	+1	5.44	5¾	Oct 00n	98:19	98:21	+2	6.20
						8½	Nov 00n	106:24	106:26	+2	6.22

Thus, the dollar and cents price of a $1,000 bond quoted as 100:01 (which means $100:\frac{1}{32}$) is $1,000.31, rounded to the nearest cent. Multiply $1,000 times 1.0003125 to get $1,000.31, the bond price times the listed price in 32nds. Enter $1,000 in memory and recall it for each multiplication.

Write your answers to each question on a separate sheet of paper.

Find the cost to the nearest cent for each $1,000 Treasury bond quoted.

1. 100.05 = _____

2. 100:03 = _____

3. 100:12 = _____

4. 100:21 = _____

5. 101:06 = _____

6. 99:31 = _____

7. 100:07 = _____

8. 99:29 = _____

9. 100:09 = _____

10. 101:08 = _____

11. 100:11 = _____

12. 99:18 = _____

13. 99:22 = _____

14. 100:31 = _____

15. 101:15 – _____

16. 99:21 = _____

17. 101:21 = _____

18. 99:18 = _____

19. 102:24 = _____

20. 100:08 = _____

21. Compare the pricing of stocks with the pricing of Treasury bonds and notes. Explain.

22. Name the cents value of $\frac{1}{32}$.

Problems 1 through 10 cover investments in stocks.

Problems 11 through 20 cover bonds.

Write your answers on the Answer Tab for Practice Test 5.

For questions in Problems 1 through 7, explain the symbols that are in the stock exchange tables.

1. Sym

2. Div

3. PE

4. Vol 100s

5. Net Chg

6. n

7. s

Define the terms in Problems 8 through 10.

8. corporation

9. shareholders

10. New York Stock Exchange

For Problems 11 through 13, name three types of bonds.

14. Explain the par value of bonds.

15. Define fixed-income securities.

Convert the following corporate bond prices, as listed in the financial pages, to the equivalent dollar and cents price per $1,000 bond.

16. $99\frac{1}{8}$

17. $104\frac{5}{8}$

18. 100

19. $101\frac{3}{8}$

20. $97\frac{7}{8}$

Problems 21 through 30 cover yields on investments.

Problems 31 through 40 cover selling price of stocks.

CORPORATE BONDS
Volume, $26,130,000

Bonds	Cur Yld	Vol	Close	Net Chg
NJBTI 7¼11	7.3	5	99⅛	− ⅜
NYTel 6¼04	6.5	25	96⅝	+ ¾
NYTel 4⅞06	5.6	11	87	+ 1⅝
NYTel 7¾06	7.7	10	100¾	...
NYTel 6s07	6.5	10	91¾	− ¼
NYTel 7½09	7 5	15	100⅝	...
NYTel 7⅜11	7.4	2	99¼	...
NYTel 7⅝23	7.6	25	99¾	...
NYTel 7s25	7.5	20	92¾	− ½

21. Name a company that is listed in the stock table.

22. A stock table in a financial newspaper lists a stock with a dividend of 2.33 and a yield of 9.0. Explain what these figures mean.

For Problems 23 through 30, find the interest rate, maturity date, and closing price per $1,000 bond for the 8 NYTEL corporation bonds listed in the table at the left. An example is given for the first bond listed.

NJBTI: $7\frac{1}{4}$%   2011 $991.25

	Interest Rate	Maturity Date	Closing Price		Interest Rate	Maturity Date	Closing Price
23.	___	___	___	**27.**	___	___	___
24.	___	___	___	**28.**	___	___	___
25.	___	___	___	**29.**	___	___	___
26.	___	___	___	**30.**	___	___	___

Define the following terms.

31. investment bankers

32. underwriter

33. prospectus

34. stockbrokers

35. SEC

In Problems 36 through 40, convert the following stock prices into dollars and cents. Round to the nearest cent.

36. $21\frac{5}{16}$

37. $18\frac{5}{8}$

38. $32\frac{3}{16}$

39. $44\frac{1}{2}$

40. $8\frac{1}{16}$

L E S S O N 30

INTEREST AND MORTGAGE INTEREST

Interest is the amount a lender charges a borrower for the use of money. To find the **simple interest** on a loan, use the formula **Interest = Principal × Rate × Time.** The formula is abbreviated $I = PRT$. The **principal** is the amount borrowed. The **rate** is the interest rate *per year.* The **time** is the period for which the money is borrowed. If the time is less than one year, it is expressed as a fraction of a year.

Remember to estimate your answers first.

Demonstration Problems

Find the annual interest on a loan of $10,000 at a simple annual interest rate of 7%.

Interest = Principal × Rate × Time

= $10,000 × .07 × 1 year

= $700

Find the interest due on the same loan after the first six months.

Interest = Principal × Rate × Time

= $10,000 × .07 × $\frac{1}{2}$ (6 months = $\frac{1}{2}$ year)

= $350

SIMPLE INTEREST VERSUS COMPOUND INTEREST

Simple interest is computed on the original amount of the loan, mortgage, or credit card balance.

Compound interest is computed periodically on the original principal plus interest earned to date. Compound interest is sometimes used on deposits in financial institutions (commercial banks, credit unions, savings and loan associations, etc.). Some interest is compounded daily; some is compounded quarterly or annually. Most compounding of interest is figured by computers. All problems in this lesson will involve simple interest.

Record your answers on the Answer Tab for Lesson 30.

For all problems in this lesson, set the Decimal Point Selector at two and the Round switch in the five/four position.

Work the demonstration problems and check Problem A before solving Problems 1 through 10. Find the simple interest on the following one-year loans.

	Principal	Annual Interest Rate	Annual Interest
A.	$ 500.00	$10\frac{3}{4}\%$	$ 53.75
1.	$1,235.00	9%	$
2.	$1,750.00	8%	$
3.	$5,245.00	$9\frac{1}{2}\%$	$
4.	$ 552.00	$8\frac{1}{2}\%$	$
5.	$2,105.00	7%	$

Find the simple interest on the following six-month loans.

	Principal	Rate	Interest
6.	$4,555.00	$12\frac{1}{2}\%$	$
7.	$ 575.00	10%	$
8.	$ 875.00	$9\frac{1}{2}\%$	$
9.	$1,000.00	9%	$
10.	$1,500.00	$8\frac{1}{2}\%$	$

MORTGAGES

A **mortgage** is a written agreement between the borrower and lender. The borrower offers property (such as a home or other building) as security (insurance) on the loan. The agreement states that the lender will become the owner of the property if the borrower does not make payments as agreed.

Demonstration Problem

Find the interest due at the end of the first month of a $25,000 mortgage loan at an annual interest rate of 10%.

$$\text{Interest} = \text{Principal} \times \text{Rate} \times \text{Time}$$

$$\$208.33 = \$25,000 \times .10 \times \frac{1}{12}$$

(NOTE: One month is $\frac{1}{12}$ of a year.)

Check Problem B and then find the interest due at the end of the first month of each mortgage loan.

Estimate $\$25,000 \times .10 \times \frac{1}{12}$ as $25,000 \times \frac{1}{10} \times \frac{1}{10} = 250$.

Record your answers on the Answer Tab for Lesson 30.

	Amount of Mortgage	Annual Interest Rate	Interest Due at End of First Month
B.	$37,500	10%	$ 312.50
11.	$29,650	9%	$
12.	$27,875	8%	$
13.	$35,580	$8\frac{1}{2}$%	$
14.	$38,990	$9\frac{1}{2}$%	$
15.	$50,000	9%	$
16.	$42,250	$10\frac{3}{4}$%	$
17.	$32,900	$9\frac{1}{2}$%	$
18.	$47,500	$8\frac{1}{2}$%	$
19.	$65,000	9%	$
20.	$49,875	10%	$

PERSONAL FINANCE COMPANY LOANS

Personal finance companies charge higher rates of interest than banks do because they take more risks. On **unsecured** (no guarantee) **loans,** personal finance companies often charge interest rates of 2% per month, which amounts to 24% per year. However, the interest is usually computed on the monthly balance due.

Demonstration Problem

Find the first quarter's interest on this unsecured loan with an interest charge of 2% per month and monthly balances as shown.

January balance	$500 at 2% = $10.00
February balance	$400 at 2% = $ 8.00
March balance	$300 at 2% = $ 6.00

Quarterly interest $24.00

Use accumulative multiplication to find the first quarter's interest on the unsecured loans in the demonstration problem, Problem C, and Problems 21 through 23. Record your answers to Problems 21 through 23 on the Answer Tab for Lesson 30.

	Month	Monthly Balance Owed	2% Monthly Interest	Quarterly Interest
C.	January	$375	$ 7.50	
	February	$325	$ 6.50	
	March	$275	$ 5.50	$ 19.50
21.	January	$495	$	
	February	$445	$	
	March	$395	$	$
22.	January	$800	$	
	February	$775	$	
	March	$750	$	$
23.	January	$900	$	
	February	$800	$	
	March	$700	$	$

CREDIT CARD FINANCE CHARGES

Credit card companies provide a convenient way to shop by lending customers money to pay for purchases. They charge interest (**finance charges**) on balances not paid by the due date. The finance charge rates are set by state governments.

Demonstration Problem

Find the finance charge and the total due at the end of the month with a $1\frac{1}{2}\%$ monthly finance charge and an unpaid balance of $169.71.

Balance	$\times$	Finance Rate	$=$ Finance Charge
$169.71	$\times$	1.5%	$= 2.55

Finance Charge	$+$	Balance	$=$ Total Due
$2.55	$+$	$169.71	$= 172.26

Work the demonstration problem, Problem D, and Problems 24 through 33. Find the monthly finance charge and the balance due at the end of the month. Record your answers to Problems 24 through 33 on the Answer Tab for Lesson 30.

	Charge Account Balance	$1\frac{1}{2}\%$ Monthly Finance Charge	Balance Plus Finance Charge
D.	$ 175.75	$ 2.64	$ 178.39
24.	$1,292.50	$	$
25.	$ 838.50	$	$
26.	$1,357.23	$	$
27.	$ 412.12	$	$
28.	$1,098.98	$	$
29.	$ 865.89	$	$
30.	$ 395.98	$	$
31.	$1,211.22	$	$
32.	$ 575.43	$	$
33.	$ 332.10	$	$

SHORT-TERM INTEREST

When interest is figured for a period of less than one year, the **banker's year** is used as the basis for computing time. The banker's year is a 360-day year. To find short-term interest for less than a year, use three-factor multiplication followed by division. The three factors multiplied are the principal, the rate, and the time (number of days). Then divide by 360 to find the interest due.

Demonstration Problem

Find the interest on a loan of $4,500 at a 9% annual interest rate for 93 days.

$$\text{Interest} = \text{Principal} \times \text{Rate} \times \text{Time}$$
$$= \$4,500 \times .09 \times \frac{93}{360}$$
$$= \$104.63$$

Check Problem E and work Problems 34 through 44.

Record your answers to Problems 34 through 44 on the Answer Tab for Lesson 30.

	Principal	Annual Interest Rate	Time	Interest
E.	$ 3,500	$8\frac{1}{2}\%$	123 days	$ 101.65
34.	$12,750	$9\frac{1}{2}\%$	90 days	$
35.	$ 8,120	10%	130 days	$
36.	$ 6,795	$9\frac{1}{2}\%$	75 days	$
37.	$15,890	$8\frac{1}{2}\%$	30 days	$
38.	$ 3,960	$7\frac{1}{2}\%$	83 days	$
39.	$16,666	7%	79 days	$
40.	$ 4,488	$9\frac{1}{4}\%$	111 days	$
41.	$12,000	$8\frac{1}{2}\%$	59 days	$
42.	$ 5,799	9%	105 days	$
43.	$ 7,778	$10\frac{1}{4}\%$	99 days	$

44. Communication   Find any two examples of interest rates and how they are used.

TRUE ANNUAL INTEREST RATE

The federal truth-in-lending law requires that a borrower be given two facts about any loan: (1) the total **installment,** or **finance charge** (interest) and (2) the *true annual interest rate.*

When interest is based on the full amount of a loan and not on the balance owed as payments are made, the borrower is actually paying an annual interest rate that is almost double the simple interest rate. This rate is the **true annual interest rate.**

Remember to estimate your answers first.

Demonstration Problem

Find the true annual interest rate on a $2,400 car loan for $2\frac{1}{2}$ years at a 10% annual interest rate with 30 monthly payments.

1. Set the Decimal Point Selector at four and use a continuous operation.

2. Find the installment charge (interest).

$$\begin{aligned} \text{Interest} &= \text{Principal} \times \text{Rate} \times \text{Time} \\ &= \$2,400 \times .10 \times 2.5 \\ &= \$600 \end{aligned}$$

This is the calculator sequence for finding the true annual interest rate.

Enter	Press	Tape
	T	0.0000 T
24	×	24.0000 ×
600	÷	600.0000 ÷
2400	÷	2400.0000 ÷
31	=	31.0000 =
		.1935

For all problems in this lesson, set the Decimal Point Selector at four and the Round switch in the five/four position. Then mentally round any dollar amounts to the nearest cent. Express percents to two decimal places.

3. To find the true annual interest rate, use this formula.

$$\text{True Annual Interest Rate} = 24 \times C \div P \div (N + 1)$$

$$= 24 \times \$600 \div \$2,400 \div (30 + 1)$$

$$= 19.35\%$$

NOTE: The symbols in the formula have the following meanings.

24 = constant with monthly payments

C = installment charge

P = principal

N = number of installments

The 24 is a *constant number* in this formula when the problem deals with monthly payment periods. It is obtained by multiplying the payment periods in one year by 2 (12 months × 2 = 24). If there were weekly payment periods, the *constant number* would be 104 (52 weeks × 2 = 104).

Find the installment charge (interest) and compute the true annual interest rate in Problems 1 through 20. Check Problems A and B before completing the problems.

Use this formula:

$$\frac{\text{True Annual}}{\text{Interest Rate}} = 24 \times C \div P \div (N + 1)$$

   24 = constant with monthly payments

   C = installment charge

   P = principal

   N = number of installments

Record your answers on the Answer Tab for Lesson 31.

	Principal	Annual Interest Rate	Time	Number of Monthly Payments	Installment Charge	True Annual Interest Rate
A.	$1,000	10 %	2 years	24	$ 200.00	19.20 %
B.	$1,500	$10\frac{1}{4}$%	1 year	12	$ 153.75	18.92 %
1.	$3,200	$9\frac{1}{2}$%	2 years	24	$ _____	_____ %
2.	$1,900	$9\frac{3}{4}$%	$2\frac{3}{4}$ years	33	$ _____	_____ %
3.	$2,200	10 %	3 years	36	$ _____	_____ %
4.	$3,400	$10\frac{3}{4}$%	$2\frac{1}{2}$ years	30	$ _____	_____ %
5.	$3,500	9 %	3 years	36	$ _____	_____ %
6.	$1,600	$9\frac{1}{2}$%	$2\frac{1}{2}$ years	30	$ _____	_____ %
7.	$2,350	10 %	2 years	24	$ _____	_____ %
8.	$4,100	9 %	$2\frac{1}{4}$ years	27	$ _____	_____ %
9.	$2,700	$10\frac{1}{2}$%	1 year	12	$ _____	_____ %
10.	$4,600	9 %	3 years	36	$ _____	_____ %

Record your answers for Problems 11 through 22 on the Answer Tab for Lesson 31.

	Principal	Annual Interest Rate	Time	Number of Monthly Payments	Installment Charge	True Annual Interest Rate
11.	$14,200	11 %	$2\frac{1}{2}$ years	30	$_____	_____ %
12.	$16,000	$10\frac{3}{4}$%	4 years	48	$_____	_____ %
13.	$14,800	$8\frac{1}{4}$%	$2\frac{1}{2}$ years	30	$_____	_____ %
14.	$ 5,200	$8\frac{1}{2}$%	3 years	36	$_____	_____ %
15.	$13,000	9 %	3 years	36	$_____	_____ %
16.	$11,200	$10\frac{1}{2}$%	$3\frac{1}{2}$ years	42	$_____	_____ %
17.	$ 4,175	10 %	2 years	24	$_____	_____ %
18.	$11,850	$9\frac{3}{4}$%	$2\frac{1}{2}$ years	30	$_____	_____ %
19.	$12,750	9 %	$1\frac{1}{2}$ years	18	$_____	_____ %
20.	$ 6,400	$10\frac{1}{2}$%	3 years	36	$_____	_____ %

21. **Communication** Explain what 24, C, P, and $(N + 1)$ represent in the true annual interest rate formula.

22. **Communication** What is the constant number in the true annual interest rate formula that deals with weekly payment periods? Explain.

INSTALLMENT BUYING

OBJECTIVE

- *Find down payment, installment price, installment charge, and percent of the list price that the installment charge represents.*

Expensive items, such as cars, furniture, and jewelry, are often bought on the *installment plan.* The buyer is usually required to make a *down payment.* The balance is then paid off in installments over a fixed period of time.

The amount paid off in installments is actually a loan by the seller to the buyer of the item. The *installment charge* is the interest paid on the loan.

Remember to estimate your answers first.

For the Demonstration Problem on page 193, set the Decimal Point Selector at four and the Round switch in the five/four position.

The **down payment** is an initial payment that is usually a percent of the list price, for example, 20% down. **Installments** are the partial payments of fixed amounts that are made periodically, usually monthly. The **installment price** is the sum of the down payment, interest, and remaining balance. The **installment charge** (or finance charge) is the amount the buyer pays over the list price. It is the seller's fee for making the loan.

The buyer must sign an installment contract, which states the number of payments and the amount of each payment. Also listed in the contract are penalties for nonpayment.

The buyer should find out the percent of the list price that the installment charge represents: the smaller the percent, the better.

Use mixed operations to solve the demonstration problem at the right.

Enter	Press	Tape	
	T	0.0000 T	
279.99	×	279.9900 ×	
.20	=	.2000 =	
		56.0000	(down payment)
	+	56.0000 +	
10	×	10.0000 ×	
26.56	=	26.5600 =	
		265.60	
	+	265.6000 +	
	S	321.6000 S	(installment price)
279.99	−	279.9900 −	
	T	41.6100 T	(installment charge)
	÷	41.6100 ÷	
279.99	=	279.9900 =	
		.1486	(14.86%)

The installment buyer would pay 14.86% more than a buyer who paid cash.

Demonstration Problem

A videocassette recorder is advertised at a list price of $279.99. It may be bought on the installment plan with a down payment of 20% of the list price and 10 equal monthly installments of $26.56 each. Find the following: (a) the amount of the down payment, (b) the installment price, (c) the installment charge, and (d) the percentage of the list price that the installment charge represents.

a.

$$\begin{array}{ccccc} \text{List} & & \text{Down Payment} & & \text{Down} \\ \text{Price} & \times & \text{Percent} & = & \text{Payment} \\ \$279.99 & \times & .20 & = & \$56.00 \end{array}$$

b.

$$\begin{array}{ccccccc} \text{Down} & & \left(\text{Number of}\right. & & \text{Each} & & \text{Installment} \\ \text{Payment} & + & \text{Installments} & \times & \left.\text{Installment}\right) & = & \text{Price} \\ \$56.00 & + & (10 & \times & \$26.56) & = & \$321.60 \end{array}$$

c.

$$\begin{array}{ccccc} \text{Installment} & & \text{List} & & \text{Installment} \\ \text{Price} & - & \text{Price} & = & \text{Charge} \\ \$321.60 & - & \$279.99 & = & \$41.61 \end{array}$$

d.

$$\begin{array}{ccccc} \text{Installment} & & \text{List} & & \text{Percent of List Price} \\ \text{Charge} & \div & \text{Price} & = & \text{Installment Charge Represents} \\ \$41.61 & \div & \$279.99 & = & 14.86\% \end{array}$$

Set the Decimal Point Selector at four and the Round switch in the five/four position for all problems in this lesson. Mentally round any dollar amounts to the nearest cent. Express percents to two decimal places.

Check Problem A and work Problems 1 through 10. In all problems find the following:

a. the amount of the down payment

b. the installment price

c. the installment (finance) charge

d. the percent of the list price that the installment charge represents

A. A color television is advertised at a list price of $549.50. It may be bought on the installment plan if a down payment of 10% of the list price is made together with 30 equal monthly installments of $18.65 each.

a. $54.95   **b.** $614.45   **c.** $64.95   **d.** 11.82%

1. A stereo system is advertised at a list price of $995. It may be bought on the installment plan if a down payment of 15% of the list price is made together with 10 equal monthly installments of $99.50 each.

2. A refrigerator is advertised at a list price of $735. It may be bought on the installment plan if a down payment of 10% of the list price is made together with 10 equal monthly installments of $75 each.

3. A diamond ring is advertised at a list price of $1,350. It may be bought on the installment plan if a down payment of 20% of the list price is made together with 12 equal monthly payments of $110.00 each.

4. A sewing machine is advertised at a list price of $450. It may be bought on the installment plan if a down payment of 25% of the list price is made together with 10 equal monthly installments of $45 each.

5. A color television is advertised at a list price of $890. It may be bought on the installment plan if a down payment of 15% of the list price is made together with 24 equal monthly installments of $40 each.

Record your answers on the Answer Tab for Lesson 32.

6. A radio is advertised at a list price of $79.99. It may be bought on the installment plan if a down payment of 25% of the list price is made together with 12 equal monthly installments of $7.00 each.

7. A piano is advertised at a list price of $2,500. It may be bought on the installment plan if a down payment of 20% of the list price is made together with 24 equal monthly installments of $115 each.

8. A swimming pool is advertised at a list price of $3,600. It may be bought on the installment plan if a down payment of 25% of the list price is made together with 24 equal monthly installments of $160 each.

9. A boat is advertised at a list price of $5,200. It may be bought on the installment plan if a down payment of $33\frac{1}{3}$% of the list price is made together with 12 equal monthly installments of $400 each.

10. Patio furniture is advertised at a list price of $2,500. It may be bought on the installment plan if a down payment of 10% of the list price is made together with 15 equal monthly installments of $160 each.

Business Application

INSTALLMENT BUYING OF A NEW CAR.

First find the total cost of the new car if you were to pay cash. Then find the installment price of the car if you took advantage of the installment plan offered.

Complete Problems 11 through 21.

List price at dealer's showroom		$14,680.00
Plus accessories:		
Power locks	$192.00	
Air conditioning	$825.00	
Power windows	$249.50	
Tinted glass	$175.50	
Trunk release	$ 50.00	
CD player	$498.00	
Total accessories		$ _____ 11.
Plus shipping charges		$ 495.00
Subtotal		$ _____ 12.
Plus a 5% sales tax on subtotal		$ _____ 13.
TOTAL CASH COST		$ _____ 14.

Remember to record your answers on the Answer Tab for Lesson 32.

Down payment of 15% on total cash cost $ _____   **15.**

Plus 36 installments at $500.00 each $ _____   **16.**

Installment price $ _____   **17.**

Less total cash cost $ _____   **18.**

Installment charge $ _____   **19.**

Percent of total cash cost that installment charge represents   _____ %   **20.**

21. Communication   Explain the following terms: (a) down payment; (b) installments; and (c) installment price.

PRORATING

Demonstration Problem

The rental expense of one company is prorated by department according to the amount of space used by each. Find the amount of the total rental expense of $220,000 charged to each department if the percent assignment according to use was as follows.

Prorating is the dividing up of an amount according to percents or a ratio between amounts. Prorating is used in preparing budgets, dividing expenses, and distributing profits.

PRORATING BY PERCENTS

A company could divide its rental expenses among its departments according to the space each used. If a department used 25% of the space, it would pay 25% of the rent.

Remember to estimate your answers first.

Department	Percent of Space Used	Rental Expense
A	25.00%	$ 55,000
B	14.30	31,460
C	11.70	25,740
D	9.50	20,900
E	39.50	86,900
TOTAL	100.00%	$ 220,000

Notice that each department is assigned a different percent according to the space it uses.

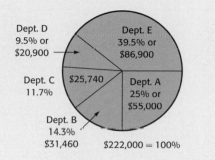

Dept. D
9.5% or
$20,900

Dept. E
39.5% or
$86,900

Dept. C
11.7%

$25,740

Dept. A
25% or
$55,000

Dept. B
14.3%

$31,460

$222,000 = 100%

The percents total 100%. The charges to the departments will total 100% of the rental expense, or $220,000.

Work the demonstration problem on your calculator. You may be able to use the $=+$ key instead of $=$ and then $+$. Set the Decimal Point Selector at two and the Round switch in the five/four position. Check your calculator manual for the method to use for accumulating constant multiplication.

1. Use constant multiplication to assign expenses to each department. The total rental expense ($220,000) is the constant factor.

2. Add the rent expenses to check that they total $220,000.

Enter	Press	Tape	
	T	0.00 T	
220,000	×	220,000 ×	
.25	=	.25 =	(percent A)
		55,000.00	(expense A)
	+	55,000.00 +	
.143	=	.143 =	(percent B)
		31,460.00	(expense B)
	+	31,460.00 +	
.117	=	.117 =	(percent C)
		25,740.00	(expense C)
	+	25,740.00 +	
.095	=	.095 =	(percent D)
		20,900.00	(expense D)
	+	20,900.00 +	
.395	=	.395 =	(percent E)
		86,900.00	(expense E)
	+	86,900.00 +	
	T	220,000.00 T	(total expense)

Check the demonstration problem and Problems A through D. Then solve Problems 1 through 20 and record your answers on the Answer Tab for Lesson 33.

A.	9.4%	$ 18,386.40
B.	20.6%	$ 40,293.60
C.	30.5%	$ 59,658.00
D.	39.5%	$ 77,262.00
	100.0%	$195,600.00

1.	23.0%	$_____
2.	30.0%	$_____
3.	25.0%	$_____
4.	22.0%	$_____
	100.0%	$ 5,600.00

5.	33.0%	$_____
6.	22.0%	$_____
7.	25.0%	$_____
8.	20.0%	$_____
	100.0%	$ 6,550.00

9.	48.0%	$_____
10.	27.0%	$_____
11.	10.0%	$_____
12.	15.0%	$_____
	100.0%	$ 7,475.00

13.	22.5%	$_____
14.	28.4%	$_____
15.	21.3%	$_____
16.	27.8%	$_____
	100.0%	$ 65,950.00

17.	25.4%	$_____
18.	27.9%	$_____
19.	30.6%	$_____
20.	16.1%	$_____
	100.0%	$ 75,000.00

PRORATING A FAMILY BUDGET

Problems 21 through 30 represent the prorated budget of a family with a total yearly budget of $35,750. Use $35,750 as the constant factor in multiplying to find the dollar allowance for each item. Check to see that the total of all items equals the total yearly budget.

Record your answers on the Answer Tab for Lesson 33.

Item	Percent Assignment	Budget
21. Food	21.7%	$ _____
22. Telephone	1.8	$ _____
23. Housing	36.9	$ _____
24. Utilities	4.0	$ _____
25. Clothing	10.1	$ _____
26. Medical and dental care	9.7	$ _____
27. Recreation	1.5	$ _____
28. Education	2.2	$ _____
29. Transportation	6.6	$ _____
30. Other expenditures	2.2	$ _____
TOTAL	100.0%	$ 35,750.00

PRORATING BY RATIOS

Sometimes prorating is expressed as the ratio between two amounts. A retail store may assign its overhead expense to each department in proportion to each department's share of total sales. Total overhead expense divided by total sales gives the constant ratio (a decimal) used to find each department's share of overhead expense.

Total Overhead Expense	÷	Total Sales	=	Constant Ratio
$138,357	÷	$475,468	=	.290991

Constant Ratio	×	Dept. A's Sales	=	Dept. A's Overhead Expense
.290991	×	$100,452	=	$29,230.63

Demonstration Problem

The overhead expense of a company is prorated by department in proportion to each department's share of the total sales. Find the amount of the total overhead expense of $138,357 charged to each department if sales were as follows.

Department	Sales	Overhead Expense
A	$ 100,452	$ 29,230.63
B	$ 82,881	$ 24,117.63
C	$ 108,775	$ 31,652.55
D	$ 85,550	$ 24,894.28
E	$ 97,810	$ 28,461.83
TOTAL	$ 475,468	$ 138,356.92*

*See the note on page 203.

NOTE: Because expense shares are rounded to two decimal places for dollars and cents, they will not always add up to the total expense. In the demonstration problem, the shares add up to $138,356.92, which is eight cents less than $138,357. To adjust for this, increase the largest share to make the totals agree. In the demonstration problem, you would add eight cents to $31,652.55 (Dept. C). Always adjust for such slight differences.

1. Find the constant ratio between overhead expense and total sales to six decimal places. Divide the overhead expense by the total sales.

$$138,357 \div 475,468 = .290991$$

2. To find each department's share of the overhead expense, set the Decimal Point Selector at two for dollars and cents and enter .290991 as the constant factor. Then multiply the constant factor by the sales of each of the five departments.

Enter	Press	Tape
	T	0.00 T
.290991	×	0.290991 ×
100,452	=	100,452 =
		29,230.63
82,881	÷	82,881 =
		24,117.63
108,775	=	108,775 =
		31,652.55
85,550	=	85,550 =
		24,894.28
97,810	=	97,810 =
		28,461.83

3. Use accumulative multiplication to total the expenses or add the amounts in a separate operation to see that they add up to the total $138,357.

Check the demonstration problem and follow the steps indicated in its solution to solve Problems 31 through 40. Record your answers on the Answer Tab for Lesson 33.

	Department	Sales	Overhead Expense
31.	F	$ 39,550	$_____
32.	G	$ 71,560	$_____
33.	H	$100,920	$_____
34.	I	$ 50,828	$_____
35.	J	$ 62,762	$_____
	TOTAL	$325,620	$64,720.00
36.	K	$ 95,632	$_____
37.	L	$ 40,760	$_____
38.	M	$130,224	$_____
39.	N	$ 54,622	$_____
40.	O	$ 69,402	$_____
	TOTAL	$390,640	$99,480.00

Set the Decimal Point Selector at four when solving Problems 41 through 51.

Problems 41 through 47 represent the various taxes collected by a state. Use constant division to find what percent of the total amount collected ($70,000,000) each type of tax represents.

In Problems 48 through 51, use constant division to find the percent of total sales each salesperson's sales represent.

Complete Problem 52.

Type of Tax	Amount Collected	Percent of Total Tax
41. Sales	$18,600,000	_____ %
42. Personal income	$ 7,400,000	_____ %
43. Alcohol	$ 2,700,000	_____ %
44. Tobacco	$ 3,800,000	_____ %
45. Gasoline	$ 8,200,000	_____ %
46. Corporation income	$15,000,000	_____ %
47. Other	$14,300,000	_____ %
TOTAL	$70,000,000	100.00%

Salesperson	Sales	Percent of Total Sales
48. R. Allan	$1,245	_____ %
49. H. Bennetto	$1,301	_____ %
50. M. Carey	$1,354	_____ %
51. A. Perez	$1,295	_____ %
TOTAL	$5,195	100.00%

52. Communication Explain the term *prorating*.

MEASUREMENT

OBJECTIVES
- *Identify the International System of Units (SI units).*
- *Convert between SI units and units of the U.S. Customary System (USCS).*

THE INTERNATIONAL SYSTEM OF UNITS (SI UNITS)

The **International System of Units** was established in 1960 as the international standard of measurement. It is a variation of the metric system. One advantage of the International System is that it is used by businesses around the world. Another advantage is that it is a decimal system.

Basic SI units of measurement and SI prefixes are shown at the right.

BASIC SI UNITS

Unit	Symbol	Quantity Measured
Meter	m	Length
Kilogram	kg	Mass
Liter	L	Capacity (Volume)

SI PREFIXES

Prefix	Symbol	Meaning
deci-	d	.1 times (one tenth of)
centi-	c	.01 times (one hundredth of)
milli-	m	.001 times (one thousandth of)
deka-	da	10 times
hecto-	h	100 times
kilo-	k	1,000 times

A DECIMAL SYSTEM.   In the International System, the units of measurement of one type (such as length) are related to each other by a power of 10. Thus, in length units, the kilometer is 1,000 times as large as the meter. The decimeter is one tenth of the meter. The prefix indicates which power of 10 is used with an SI unit. Memorize the basic units and the prefixes shown above before you proceed any further in this lesson.

BASIC AND DERIVED UNITS.   In the International System, the meter, gram, and liter form the basis of the many derived units. Both types of units are used for measuring different types of quantities. Study the most commonly used units shown at the right until you can think of measurement in terms of them.

SOME UNITS DERIVED FROM PREFIXES AND BASIC UNITS

Unit	Symbol	Value
decigram	dg	.1 gram
centiliter	cl	.01 liter
millimeter	mm	.001 meter
dekaliter	dal	10 liters
hectometer	hm	100 meters
kilogram	kg	1,000 grams

APPROXIMATE EQUIVALENTS OF COMMONLY USED SI UNITS

Type of Quantity Measured	Unit	Approximate Equivalent
length	meter	1 yard
	kilometer	$\frac{1}{2}$ mile
	millimeter	the thickness of a paper match
weight	gram	the weight of two paper clips
	kilogram	2 pounds
	milligram	the weight of a grain of salt
capacity	liter	1 quart
	kiloliter	2 bathtubs of water
	milliliter	$\frac{1}{4}$ teaspoonful

Remember to estimate your answers first.

Check Problem A and then solve Problems 1 through 19. Record your answers on the Answer Tab for Lesson 34. Be sure you can answer all 19 questions before you continue the rest of the lesson.

U.S. CUSTOMARY SYSTEM (USCS) AND CONVERSION TABLES

Although the U.S. Customary System is still used for everyday measurement in the United States, it will probably be replaced by the International System. Meanwhile, it is useful to know how to convert SI units into USCS units and vice versa.

USCS and SI units were developed independently. Therefore, conversion factors between these systems follow no pattern. Tables such as those on the following pages list the most common conversion factors.

A. A centimeter is what part of a meter?   .01

1. A decimeter is what part of a meter?

2. How many meters are there in a kilometer?

3. A millimeter is what part of a meter?

4. How many meters are there in a hectometer?

5. How many meters are there in a dekameter?

6. What basic SI unit measures weight?

7. What basic SI unit measures capacity?

8. What basic SI unit measures length?

9. A centiliter is what part of a liter?

10. A decigram is what part of a gram?

What are the approximate SI equivalents of the following?

11. 1 quart

12. The weight of a grain of salt

13. 1 yard

14. $\frac{1}{4}$ teaspoonful

15. 2 pounds

16. $\frac{1}{2}$ mile

17. The weight of two paper clips

18. 2 bathtubs of water

19. The thickness of a paper match

CONVERTING UNITS OF LENGTH. You can convert units of length from one system to the other by using a conversion table such as the one shown at the right.

Demonstration Problem

To convert meters to feet (SI):

$$20 \text{ meters} = ? \text{ feet}$$
$$3.281 \times 20 = 65.62$$

Since 1 meter equals 3.281 feet, 20 meters equals 65.62 feet (3.281×20).

To convert feet to meters (USCS):

$$65.62 \text{ feet} = ? \text{ meters}$$
$$65.62 \times 3.05 = 20.0141$$

Since 1 foot equals .305 meter, then 65.62 feet equals about 20 meters ($65.62 \times .305$).

For working all problems using the conversion tables, set the Decimal Point Selector at three and the Round switch in the five/four position.

Check Problems B and C before completing Problems 20 through 27. Record your answers on the Answer Tab for Lesson 34.

CONVERSION TABLE FOR LENGTH

SI to USCS Units		USCS to SI Units
1 meter = { 1.094 yards / 3.281 feet / 39.37 inches		1 yard = .914 meter
		1 foot = .305 meter
		1 inch = 2.54 centimeters
1 kilometer = .62 mile		1 mile = 1.609 kilometers

B. 605 meters = ? feet
1,985.005 feet
20. 4 meters = ? inches
21. 40 feet = ? meters
22. 15 miles = ? kilometers
23. 42 meters = ? yards

C. 30 miles = ? kilometers
48.27 kilometers
24. 6 inches = ? centimeters
25. 8 yards = ? meters
26. 10 meters = ? feet
27. 5 kilometers = ? miles

CONVERTING UNITS OF CAPACITY.

Similarly, to convert units of capacity from one system to the other, use a conversion table such as the one shown at the right.

Demonstration Problem

To convert liters to gallons (SI):

$$20 \text{ liters} = ? \text{ gallons}$$
$$.264 \times 20 = 5.28$$

To convert gallons to liters (USCS):

$$5.28 \text{ gallons} = ? \text{ liters}$$
$$5.28 \times 3.785 = 19.9848 \text{ or } 20$$

Check Problems D and E before completing Problems 28 through 35.

Record your answers on the Answer Tab for Lesson 34.

CONVERSION TABLE FOR CAPACITY

SI to USCS Units		USCS to SI	
1 liter =	$\begin{cases} 1.057 \text{ quarts} \\ .264 \text{ gallon} \end{cases}$	1 quart =	.946 liter
		1 gallon =	3.785 liters
1 milliliter =	.0338 fluid ounce	1 fluid ounce =	29.57 milliliters

D. 1.50 liters = ? quarts
1.5855 quarts
28. 25 milliliters = ? fluid ounces
29. 40 fluid ounces = ? milliliters
30. 4 quarts = ? liters
31. 8 liters = ? quarts

E. 4 gallons = ? liters
15.14 liters
32. 5 gallons = ? liters
33. 8 liters = ? gallons
34. 100 liters = ? gallons
35. 25 quarts = ? liters

CONVERTING UNITS OF WEIGHT.

For converting units of weight from one system to the other, use a conversion table such as the one shown at the right.

Demonstration Problem

To convert kilograms to pounds (SI):

$$4 \text{ kilograms} = ? \text{ pounds}$$
$$2.205 \times 4 = 8.82$$

To convert pounds to kilograms (USCS):

$$8.82 \text{ pounds} = ? \text{ kilograms}$$
$$8.82 \times .4536 = 4.000752 \text{ or } 4$$

Check Problems F and G before completing Problems 36 through 43.

Problems 44 through 53 are a review of what you have learned about converting units of measurement from one system to the other.

Record your answers on the Answer Tab for Lesson 34.

CONVERSION TABLE FOR WEIGHT

SI to USCS Units		USCS to SI	
1 gram	= .0353 ounce	1 ounce	= 28.3 grams
1 kilogram	= 2.205 pounds	1 pound	$-\begin{cases} 453.6 \text{ grams} \\ .4536 \text{ kilogram} \end{cases}$
1 metric ton	= 2,205 pounds	1 ton (English)	$=\begin{cases} 907.18 \text{ kilograms} \\ .9 \text{ metric ton} \end{cases}$

F. 10 grams = ? ounces
.353 ounce

36. 30 ounces = ? grams
37. 2 tons (English) = ? metric tons
38. 2 pounds = ? grams
39. 15 kilograms = ? pounds

G. 7 pounds = ? kilograms
3.1752 kilograms

40. 20 pounds = ? kilograms
41. 14 grams = ? ounces
42. 50 grams = ? ounces
43. 6 tons (English) = ? kilograms

44. ? liters = 3 quarts
45. ? yards = 21 meters
46. 606 miles = ? kilometers
47. 7.2 kilograms = ? pounds
48. 30 pounds = ? grams

49. ? fluid ounces = 600 milliliters
50. 3 milliliters = ? fluid ounces
51. ? inches = 12 meters
52. 24 tons (English) = ? metric tons
53. 66.8 grams = ? ounces

Interest and Proration

Find the first quarter's interest on this unsecured loan with an interest charge of 2% per month and monthly balances of $500, $400, and $300 (demonstration problem from page 185). Use the following sequence.

500 ☒ 2 % ═ 10 STO 400 ☒ 2 % ═ 8 SUM 300 ☒ 2 % ═ SUM RCL 2nd [MEM] ═ 24

To find the finance charge and the total due at the end of the month for a 1.5% finance charge and an unpaid balance of $169.71 (as in the demonstration problem on page 186), use the following sequence.

169 ⨀ 71 STO ☒ 1 ⨀ 5 % ═ 2.54565 SUM RCL 2nd [MEM] ═ 172.25565

The finance charge is $2.54 and the total due is $172.26.

Write your answers on a separate sheet of paper.

Find the first quarter's interest on this unsecured loan with an interest rate of 2.5% per month and monthly balances as shown.

1. $600, $500, $400
2. $725, $650, $575

Find the monthly finance charge and total due at the end of the month for a 1.8% monthly finance charge and unpaid balances as shown. Round answers to the nearest cent.

3. $237.89   4. $178.16

5. Find the true annual interest rate on a $12,000 car loan for 4 years at a 9% annual interest rate with 48 monthly payments.

6. A color inkjet printer has a list price of $385.99. It may be bought on the installment plan with a down payment of 25% of the list price and 12 equal monthly installments of $28.11 each. Find the down payment, the installment price, the installment charge, and the percent of the list price that the installment charge represents.

To find the true annual interest rate on a loan of $2,400 for 2.5 years at a 10% annual interest rate with 30 monthly payments (demonstration problem from pages 188–189), use the true annual interest rate formula and the following sequence.

2,400 $\boxed{\times}$ 10 $\boxed{\%}$ $\boxed{\times}$ 2 $\boxed{.}$ 5 $\boxed{\times}$ 24 $\boxed{\div}$ 2,400 $\boxed{\div}$ 31 $\boxed{=}$ .1935

The true annual interest rate is 19.35%.

For the demonstration problem on page 193, find the down payment, installment price, installment charge, and percent of list price that the installment charge represents. Use the following sequence of numbers and keys.

279 $\boxed{.}$ 99 $\boxed{\times}$ 20 $\boxed{\%}$ $\boxed{=}$ 55.998 $\boxed{\text{STO}}$ 10 $\boxed{\times}$ 26 $\boxed{.}$ 56 $\boxed{+}$ $\boxed{\text{RCL}}$ $\boxed{\text{2nd}}$ [MEM] $\boxed{=}$ 321.598 $\boxed{-}$ 279 $\boxed{.}$ 99 $\boxed{=}$ 41.608 $\boxed{\div}$ 279 $\boxed{.}$ 99 $\boxed{=}$ .148605307

The down payment is $56.00, the installment price is $321.60, the installment charge is $41.61, and the percent of list price that the installment charge represents is 14.86%.

Practice Test 6

Problems 1 through 6 review simple interest, the true annual interest rate, and installment buying. Set the Decimal Point Selector at four and the Round switch in the five/four position. Then mentally round any dollar amounts to the nearest cent.

$$\text{True Annual Interest Rate} = 24 \times C \div P \div (N + 1)$$

24 = constant
C = installment (finance) charge
P = principal
N = total number of payments

Record your answers on the Answer Tab for Practice Test 6.

1. Find the simple annual interest on a depositor's bank balance of $12,555 if the annual interest rate is $\frac{3}{8}$%.

2. What is the quarterly simple interest on an unsecured loan with a $1\frac{1}{4}$% monthly interest rate if the balance owed in January was $2,340; in February, $2,100; and in March, $1,860?

3. Find the simple interest on a $5,000 loan for 75 days at an annual interest rate of $6\frac{3}{8}$%. (Use 360 for the number of days in a full year.)

4. What is the true annual interest rate on a $9,000 car loan for $3\frac{1}{2}$ years at a 6% annual interest rate with 42 monthly payments?

5. What is the true annual interest rate on a $5,000 car loan for 2 years at an annual interest rate of $5\frac{3}{4}$% with 24 monthly payments?

6. A color television is advertised at a list price of $899. It may be bought on the installment plan if a down payment of 25% of the list price is made followed by 10 equal monthly installments of $90 each. Find the amount of the down payment, the installment price, the installment charge, and the percent of the list price that the installment charge represents.

Complete Problems 7 through 21, which review pro-rating by percents. Set the Decimal Point Selector at two and the Round switch to the five/four position.

Record your answers on the Answer Tab for Practice Test 6.

7.	22%	$_____
8.	11%	$_____
9.	33%	$_____
10.	19%	$_____
11.	15%	$_____
	100%	$565,565.00

12.	12%	$_____
13.	10%	$_____
14.	7%	$_____
15.	6%	$_____
16.	5%	$_____
17.	4%	$_____
18.	3%	$_____
19.	11%	$_____
20.	18%	$_____
21.	24%	$_____
	100%	$250,750.00

Complete Problems 22 through 26, which review pro-rating by ratios.

Record your answers on the Answer Tab for Practice Test 6.

The overhead expense of one company is prorated by department in proportion to each department's share of the total sales. Find the amount of the total overhead expense of $950,000.00 charged to each department if sales were as follows. Round your answers to the nearest whole dollar.

	Department	Sales	Overhead Expense
22.	A	$1,400,000	$_____
23.	B	$1,800,000	$_____
24.	C	$ 800,000	$_____
25.	D	$1,000,000	$_____
26.	E	$ 1,600,000	$_____
	TOTAL	$6,600,000	$ 950,000.00

Complete Problems 27 through 32, which are a review of conversion between SI and USCS units.

Set the Decimal Point Selector at four and the Round switch in the five/four position.

Complete Problems 33 through 40, which are a review of SI units and do not require the use of your calculator.

Record your answers on the Answer Tab for Practice Test 6.

After you have completed Practice Test 6, check with your instructor about taking Test 6.

27. If 1 meter equals 3.281 feet, how many feet are there in 150 meters?

28. If 1 quart equals .946 liter, how many liters are there in 3 quarts?

29. If 1 kilometer equals .62 mile, how many miles are there in 2.5 kilometers?

30. If 1 milliliter equals .0338 fluid ounce, how many fluid ounces are there in 50 milliliters?

31. If 1 pound equals .4536 kilogram, how many kilograms are there in 5 pounds?

32. If 1 gram equals .0353 ounce, how many ounces are there in 15 grams?

33. How many centimeters are there in a meter?

34. How many millimeters are there in a meter?

35. How many liters are there in a dekaliter?

36. A centimeter is what part of a meter?

37. A gram is what part of a kilogram?

38. How many liters are there in a hectoliter?

39. A decigram is what part of a gram?

40. A centiliter is what part of a liter?

41. **Communication**   Show an SI unit for length.

PROGRESS TEST 1

The 5 key is in the center of the figure keyboard. When your middle finger rests on the 5 key, you can easily reach all the other numeric keys with the proper fingers. As you know, three keys should be pressed with the index finger: 7 , 4 and 1 ; three keys should be pressed with the middle finger: 8 , 5 , and 2 ; and three keys should be pressed with the ring finger: 9 , 6 , and 3 . The 0 key should be pressed with the side of the right thumb and the + bar should be pressed with the little finger.

These addition problems stress reaching to the corner keys: 7 , 1 , 9 , and 3 . By now you should be able to solve all ten addition problems by touch in ten minutes or less.

1.	2.	3.	4.	5.
575	15	159	335	753
75	115	95	533	159
75	145	559	563	759
547	15	659	635	153
774	515	95	53	574
57	551	995	963	75
757	451	595	356	119
747	145	959	35	115
757	541	59	35	91
775	51	519	539	357
5,139	2,544	4,694	4,047	3,155

6.	7.	8.	9.	10.
75	175	569	535	15
750	511	95	35	75
577	541	795	563	39
575	145	559	533	10
755	15	779	153	19
70	751	59	365	95
147	175	195	35	79
75	515	795	350	50
705	150	975	36	45
177	745	95	339	59
3,906	3,723	4,916	2,944	486

By now you should be able to solve all ten addition problems by touch in ten minutes or less. Make sure that you are using the proper fingers and not looking at the keyboard.

1.	2.	3.	4.	5.
35	470	199	201	255
775	956	3,773	30	375
566	680	288	3,313	25
520	1,275	107	827	89
1,125	320	398	932	2,198
89	85	981	370	1,250
325	145	782	172	655
3,450	310	1,100	319	7
8,230	590	37	973	5,500
45	365	91	298	3,450
15,160	5,196	7,756	7,435	13,804

Continue to work these problems until you are able to arrive at the correct answers within ten minutes.

6.	7.	8.	9.	10.
425	91	214	3,300	856
710	275	423	6,032	18
680	2,360	337	43	117
159	280	229	275	3,960
950	587	54	1,893	1,008
690	500	557	48	8,234
119	980	146	788	218
964	1,124	748	79	64
687	163	2,138	10	57
250	94	540	5,689	85
5,634	6,454	5,386	18,157	14,617

PROGRESS TEST 3

Add these amounts without looking at the keyboard. Remember that if you constantly take your eyes from the printed page to locate the keys, you will reduce your operating speed and increase the chance of error because you will have to find your place again in every problem. By now you should be able to solve all ten addition problems by touch in ten minutes or less.

Set the Decimal Point Selector in the Add-Mode position or at two for adding dollars and cents.

1.	2.	3.	4.	5.
$ 75.40	$ 12.20	$ 97.45	$ 29.70	$ 10.00
37.62	45.00	54.65	37.01	28.85
10.51	78.80	23.56	81.91	69.50
78.00	96.50	25.40	17.93	82.25
45.60	84.15	14.50	28.07	42.75
40.25	85.00	36.66	71.20	75.50
98.50	85.25	59.95	93.00	20.30
75.55	35.50	87.55	27.00	87.95
59.00	14.55	88.25	73.30	21.55
73.20	36.50	11.25	10.00	54.00
$593.63	$573.45	$499.22	$469.12	$492.65

Continue to work these problems until you are able to arrive at the correct answers within 10 minutes.

6.	7.	8.	9.	10.
$ 656.30	$ 32.55	$ 612.25	$ 495.00	$ 14.95
73.20	579.90	443.20	38.50	45.20
92.03	31.15	131.05	3.50	119.70
59.75	12.37	9.95	17.75	78.45
468.45	4.45	.50	162.50	4.60
9.80	277.25	39.00	.65	2.75
29.04	.60	.07	78.95	125.00
3.95	46.50	549.65	428.50	168.50
15.59	32.75	704.15	25.25	1.75
77.98	118.60	172.25	56.65	80.45
$1,486.09	$1,136.12	$2,662.07	$1,307.25	$641.35

PROGRESS TEST 4

The [5] key (the center key) and the [7], [8], and [9] keys are emphasized in these touch addition problems. You should not have any difficulty entering the amounts without looking at the keys because the lower rows of keys and the [0] key are not used.

Set the Decimal Point Selector at zero to add whole numbers.

1.	2.	3.	4.	5.
55	595	575	57	557
775	885	854	598	745
588	875	4,578	8,556	6,675
758	5	77	75	4,745
575	445	5,985	4,495	595
889	776	87,894	5,578	4,589
585	595	8,545	56,775	55,898
59	995	659	975	884
845	986	547	545	695
965	95	7,549	9,467	4,986
6,094	6,252	117,263	87,121	80,369

Continue to work these problems until you are able to arrive at the correct answers within ten minutes.

6.	7.	8.	9.	10.
75	588	59	789	4,458
5,675	85	95	995	5,695
788	98	4,595	699	7,845
7,987	89	8,898	7,698	8,956
9,575	7,886	9,956	5,577	8,754
8,754	4,885	695	598	4,975
4,578	5,678	99	475	8,847
775	4,988	8,759	8,995	5,489
77,964	6,788	6,994	4,598	5,475
4,785	9,598	8,969	9,487	6,995
77	88	6,798	5,975	5,987
4,775	698	95	6,497	788
6,789	846	5,989	8,467	9,875
7,457	9,875	985	4,578	775
78	889	975	9,875	8,945
140,132	53,079	63,961	75,303	93,859

PROGRESS TEST 5

The 0 , 1 , 2 , and 3 keys are emphasized in these touch addition problems. You should have no difficulty entering the amounts without looking at the keys because the top row of keys is not used.

Set the Decimal Point Selector at zero to add whole numbers.

1.	2.	3.	4.	5.
512	632	5,012	1,512	5,612
5,421	3,365	6,031	3,362	3,403
310	325	2,530	241	2,660
4,101	2,236	122	4,503	4,533
1,120	3,032	2,260	610	210
4,114	1,303	521	111	5,612
3,403	1,003	3,041	630	105
1,122	1,202	4,105	4,523	4,302
2,021	2,122	310	3,630	3,314
1,212	3,221	51	305	2,000
23,336	18,441	23,983	19,427	31,751

Continue to work these problems until you are able to arrive at the correct answers within ten minutes.

6.	7.	8.	9.	10.
1,230	502	145	2,233	1,152
404	4,412	630	4,410	503
2,015	3,425	405	11,215	3,200
342	35	2,402	4,612	52
2,414	123	110	2,265	101,300
331	3,123	3,111	1,221	403
4,000	350	640	2,150	2,650
345	1,040	115	50	325
1,050	210	101,225	530	5,500
3,350	2,250	4,000	300	345
215	500	1,100	2,450	2,150
2,500	2,550	2,220	520	512
650	2,060	3,635	10,055	12,320
501	402	610	120	1,040
125	325	412	3,301	1,322
19,472	21,307	120,760	45,432	132,774

PROGRESS TEST 6

These problems give additional practice in using all the numbers on the keyboard. By now you should be able to solve all 12 addition problems by touch in ten minutes or less.

Set the Decimal Point Selector in the Add-Mode position or at two.

1.	2.	3.	4.	5.	6.
.43	1.39	1.55	.79	1.49	.40
.77	.32	1.20	.97	.69	.48
.32	.55	.63	1.41	1.15	1.49
.43	.57	.32	.24	.59	2.98
1.89	.39	.47	1.29	1.70	.89
.33	1.27	.47	.35	.79	.62
2.22	.69	.55	.35	.49	1.03
1.45	.22	3.24	1.69	1.79	2.29
.62	2.09	2.20	.47	.78	.55
1.45	1.45	3.75	1.20	.69	.47
.79	.96	.41	1.37	1.25	3.25
2.40	.32	1.89	.55	1.59	.33
9.70	1.37	.33	.98	.78	.33
4.01	1.19	.66	1.31	.49	2.45
.31	1.10	1.19	1.45	1.15	1.75
27.12	13.88	18.86	14.42	15.42	19.31

Continue to work these problems until you are able to arrive at the correct answers within ten minutes.

7.	8.	9.	10.	11.	12.
.69	.37	.89	1.39	1.75	.29
1.59	.39	.33	1.09	.37	1.00
2.70	1.47	.59	.39	.52	.39
1.79	.45	.69	1.49	1.49	.29
1.19	.55	2.29	.65	.89	1.19
.31	1.59	1.89	.79	.79	1.89
.39	2.69	1.29	.59	1.19	1.99
.39	2.99	2.29	1.09	1.59	1.00
.57	.69	.87	1.59	1.89	.59
.69	1.29	2.99	.29	1.39	.99
1.22	.63	.79	.89	.59	1.89
1.05	1.39	1.19	1.99	1.39	.49
1.10	1.09	1.39	1.89	.69	1.39
2.95	1.19	1.09	.59	1.49	1.79
.47	.79	.79	1.99	.99	.89
17.10	17.57	19.37	16.71	17.02	16.07

PROGRESS TEST 7

The amounts in these addition problems are taken from bank statements. By now you should be able to solve all ten addition problems by touch and check some of them in ten minutes.

Set the Decimal Point Selector in the Add-Mode position or at two.

1.	2.	3.	4.	5.
$100.00	$3,850.00	$ 34.95	$ 21.88	$ 6.00
1.53	37.41	2.00	2,253.51	10.00
25.00	100.00	5.00	107.50	100.00
8.32	3.00	62.50	204.75	45.00
33.05	9.44	8.50	228.10	7.50
5.00	52.50	10.94	5.00	200.00
2.00	22.26	32.61	45.00	95.00
25.00	33.92	150.00	12.38	6.29
10.00	5.00	5.00	42.54	771.05
5.00	6.85	50.00	10.00	521.75
79.25	51.79	49.19	3.00	5.00
40.00	3.00	5.00	25.00	45.00
525.00	37.80	302.50	100.00	100.00
2.00	100.00	49.22	173.00	10.00
5.00	4.75	200.00	5.00	6.90
3.18	50.00	3.00	87.84	5.00
$869.33	$4,367.72	$970.41	$3,324.50	$1,934.49

Continue to work these problems until you are able to arrive at the correct answers within ten minutes.

6.	7.	8.	9.	10.
$ 13.94	$ 78.78	$ 4.66	$ 200.00	$ 50.00
100.00	10.00	46.45	3.00	10.00
31.10	14.00	20.80	529.15	10.00
15.00	27.20	22.20	45.00	858.39
3.00	2,350.95	9.00	15.20	37.55
125.00	5.69	25.00	67.20	16.05
6.60	50.00	100.00	5.00	10.10
100.00	17.80	5.00	7.50	3.00
10.00	100.00	24.90	19.75	10.00
30.04	30.08	5.00	100.00	60.00
15.20	25.50	46.73	2,278.43	25.00
12.50	18.98	29.48	46.25	5.00
29.00	7.32	10.00	379.20	9.56
1,000.00	5.00	200.00	6.85	209.75
18.00	25.00	5.00	2.14	20.00
314.30	45.00	150.00	45.00	6.85
$1,823.68	$2,811.30	$704.22	$3,749.67	$1,341.25

By now you should be able to solve all ten addition problems by touch and check some of them in ten minutes.

Set the Decimal Point Selector in the Add-Mode position or at two for adding dollars and cents.

1.	2.	3.	4.	5.
$ 36.54	$ .15	$ 64.93	$ 6.65	$ 54.50
6.38	3.85	.39	9.07	440.10
5.95	77.96	79.70	47.82	65.50
46.81	33.16	43.32	6.45	96.03
35.68	124.84	28.65	33.90	7.70
23.24	5.95	59.63	111.80	10.85
11.15	.72	11.47	88.45	.45
9.17	44.69	.83	4.96	455.52
84.65	52.28	6.95	32.08	78.53
77.52	22.56	27.25	63.50	10.25
8.85	9.20	44.50	78.50	33.35
73.95	206.80	111.75	82.45	3.95
10.65	77.50	12.45	10.80	15.45
47.15	3.75	4.55	8.25	.69
78.10	15.30	22.10	6.40	112.75
12.49	188.60	160.70	1.40	42.65
5.65	455.40	100.05	12.50	.10
9.98	.35	78.55	211.25	20.00
228.80	7.65	11.50	107.39	275.00
55.06	112.05	.50	7.00	4.70
$867.77	$1,442.76	$869.77	$930.62	$1,728.07

Continue to work these problems until you are able to arrive at the correct answers within ten minutes.

6.	7.	8.	9.	10.
$ .89	$ .95	$ 7.25	$ 4.58	$ 46.05
21.01	7.00	15.50	6.95	9.50
14.45	201.60	6.39	35.85	10.00
76.39	22.50	25.28	76.55	26.50
1.25	7.05	43.25	4.99	302.50
406.11	8.95	206.40	121.19	21.89
.50	11.25	.65	8.87	6.65
36.59	.75	162.75	406.99	.49
7.60	20.00	20.01	110.45	1.05
545.00	12.96	296.00	8.60	24.50
32.30	439.60	27.30	.66	.45
86.10	9.56	33.46	93.15	.20
19.66	60.25	75.45	305.06	12.50
7.50	79.40	200.70	66.35	22.50
106.57	42.25	.39	239.15	34.50
39.05	582.30	.87	.33	56.75
3.90	6.67	11.15	68.50	211.26
101.50	120.00	2.36	74.25	132.65
4.95	770.70	504.75	34.60	21.37
25.00	3.30	5.44	2.57	607.95
$1,536.32	$2,407.04	$1,645.35	$1,669.64	$1,549.26

PROGRESS TEST 9

By now you should be able to solve all ten addition problems by touch within ten minutes.

Set the Decimal Point Selector in the Add-Mode position or at two for adding dollars and cents.

1.	2.	3.	4.	5.
$ 25.00	$ 21.19	$ 50.80	$ 42.35	$ 5.00
50.00	2.09	6.35	86.02	8.94
15.00	7.98	43.05	6.65	50.00
35.00	15.95	8.90	30.50	68.33
55.00	31.50	51.75	36.18	3.00
22.50	12.77	9.50	22.30	16.80
3.75	8.79	38.55	38.10	100.00
1.25	21.98	4.75	6.60	5.00
2.95	22.50	50.08	80.75	97.87
29.95	110.75	26.20	14.46	22.78
20.00	65.00	44.35	7.40	2.00
100.00	19.98	.98	40.25	73.00
.50	66.95	20.95	1.71	3.68
10.50	5.00	41.15	88.10	13.50
12.75	25.00	25.50	4.75	100.00
2.25	20.00	4.25	50.65	25.00
32.25	2.25	1.03	4.77	.50
4.50	.50	17.40	20.50	16.25
1.75	22.50	59.00	1.95	.95
14.95	47.75	52.20	3.18	4.66
$439.85	$530.43	$556.74	$587.17	$617.26

Continue to work these problems until you are able to arrive at the correct answers within ten minutes.

6.	7.	8.	9.	10.
$ 22.20	$ 8.07	$ 94.75	$ .69	$ 7.05
73.77	45.46	5.86	9.72	67.51
39.04	21.54	89.93	38.96	33.28
16.25	3.56	8.75	6.40	.36
18.00	38.72	64.82	44.12	12.47
30.00	48.41	83.79	5.72	84.31
263.82	53.98	23.63	88.84	8.21
3.00	1.69	18.15	.60	.65
45.00	.84	1.88	96.25	38.28
.20	72.35	7.50	44.98	2.12
5.25	95.45	56.36	11.48	4.21
50.00	13.50	39.89	22.69	38.01
6.85	67.81	1.56	2.95	75.08
35.00	3.37	5.38	568.45	44.65
.65	29.96	48.46	.20	21.50
52.90	216.34	.91	77.06	60.50
29.17	.85	75.32	360.05	50.00
15.39	88.29	67.25	3.50	100.00
64.87	.62	66.50	22.21	25.00
3.50	68.11	57.07	219.50	363.00
74.74	.49	93.30	1.65	9.98
15.00	15.41	1.19	24.39	81.31
5.58	78.28	60.55	7.65	5.90
4.60	137.13	3.15	19.07	7.17
1.33	8.11	96.80	38.10	9.14
$876.11	$1,118.34	$1,072.75	$1,715.23	$1,149.69

By now you should be able to solve all ten addition problems by touch in ten minutes or less.

Set the Decimal Point Selector in the Add-Mode position or at two for adding dollars and cents.

1.	2.	3.	4.	5.
$ 87.35	$ 21.40	$ 52.83	$ 60.69	$ 18.00
46.70	31.15	76.25	14.45	22.15
19.95	44.11	17.95	86.35	26.50
33.20	72.65	31.45	30.90	73.75
43.75	51.25	48.90	81.10	97.26
3.98	39.95	22.31	10.55	63.90
42.01	56.25	4.13	86.65	20.35
41.65	12.50	33.95	66.50	25.50
241.08	71.69	55.56	27.65	53.40
36.96	15.67	69.50	40.21	59.79
34.72	43.44	88.88	67.05	70.25
69.98	90.20	57.85	69.30	98.20
26.89	3.95	254.35	33.70	63.85
86.62	37.25	27.75	11.85	16.60
151.10	219.79	14.56	31.06	2.61
94.05	41.98	92.85	40.59	30.60
89.75	80.00	25.60	44.36	83.15
14.50	57.29	9.25	13.00	195.05
80.86	25.49	48.44	55.09	67.76
52.15	38.00	23.65	30.75	39.60
$1,297.25	$1,054.01	$1,056.01	$901.80	$1,128.27

Continue to work these problems until you are able to arrive at the correct answers within ten minutes.

6.	7.	8.	9.	10.
$ 15.00	$ 26.80	$ 25.60	$ 200.00	$ 92.54
27.68	38.25	28.00	1.53	67.27
20.00	100.00	62.30	25.00	58.95
33.62	678.99	9.48	8.32	25.90
3.00	425.22	32.50	33.05	20.90
25.00	4.79	125.00	69.25	75.30
100.00	87.11	30.98	16.65	5.05
390.97	1.76	750.00	50.00	678.40
12.00	9.56	3.43	425.00	65.62
50.00	99.82	15.00	10.00	86.40
5.00	30.98	53.59	13.94	225.03
9.30	25.50	20.00	31.10	36.00
50.00	72.02	5.00	15.00	3.09
250.00	14.00	2.31	125.00	9.72
6.60	5.94	10.45	314.30	228.93
75.00	28.36	32.92	50.00	86.39
15.55	2.00	4.68	32.50	96.15
525.00	43.42	100.00	11.25	1.91
3.00	6.60	9.36	12.50	575.00
77.48	424.00	577.00	19.00	12.96
125.00	229.64	786.73	3.00	315.50
35.73	62.50	10.00	29.92	5.80
50.00	15.20	50.66	3.18	7.95
25.00	648.64	298.34	40.04	748.06
22.20	28.44	62.29	75.00	49.20
$1,952.13	$3,109.54	$3,105.62	$1,614.53	$3,578.02

26. _____

27. _____

28. _____

29. _____

30. _____

31. _____

32. _____

33. _____

34. _____

35. _____

36. _____

37. _____

38. _____

39. _____

40. _____

41. _____

Answer Tab
Lesson 34

NAME/DATE _____

28. _____
29. _____
30. _____
31. _____
32. _____
33. _____
34. _____
35. _____
36. _____
37. _____
38. _____
39. _____
40. _____
41. _____
42. _____
43. _____
44. _____
45. _____
46. _____
47. _____
48. _____
49. _____
50. _____
51. _____
52. _____
53. _____

1. _____
2. _____
3. _____
4. _____
5. _____
6. _____
7. _____
8. _____
9. _____
10. _____
11. _____
12. _____
13. _____
14. _____
15. _____
16. _____
17. _____
18. _____
19. _____
20. _____
21. _____
22. _____
23. _____
24. _____
25. _____
26. _____
27. _____

Answer Tab
Practice Test 6

NAME/DATE _____

1. _____
2. _____
3. _____
4. _____
5. _____
6. _____
7. _____
8. _____
9. _____
10. _____
11. _____
12. _____
13. _____
14. _____
15. _____
16. _____
17. _____
18. _____
19. _____
20. _____
21. _____
22. _____
23. _____
24. _____
25. _____

(over)

8. _____
9. _____
10. _____
11. _____
12. _____
13. _____
14. _____
15. _____
16. _____
17. _____
18. _____
19. _____
20. _____
21. _____

29. _____
30. _____
31. _____
32. _____
33. _____
34. _____
35. _____
36. _____
37. _____
38. _____
39. _____
40. _____
41. _____
42. _____
43. _____
44. _____
45. _____
46. _____
47. _____
48. _____
49. _____
50. _____
51. _____
52. _____

Answer Tab
Lesson 32

NAME/DATE _____

1.

2.

3.

4.

5.

6.

7.

(over)

Answer Tab
Lesson 33

NAME/DATE _____

1.
2.
3.
4.
5.
6.
7.
8.
9.
10.
11.
12.
13.
14.
15.
16.
17.
18.
19.
20.
21.
22.
23.
24.
25.
26.
27.
28.

(over)

38. _____
39. _____
40. _____
41. _____
42. _____
43. _____
44. _____

15. _____
16. _____
17. _____
18. _____
19. _____
20. _____
21. _____
22. _____

Answer Tab
Lesson 30

NAME/DATE _____

23. _____
_____
_____
24. _____
25. _____
26. _____
27. _____
28. _____
29. _____
30. _____
31. _____
32. _____
33. _____
34. _____
35. _____
36. _____
37. _____

1. _____
2. _____
3. _____
4. _____
5. _____
6. _____
7. _____
8. _____
9. _____
10. _____
11. _____
12. _____
13. _____
14. _____
15. _____
16. _____
17. _____
18. _____
19. _____
20. _____
21. _____
22. _____

(over)

Answer Tab
Lesson 31

NAME/DATE _____

1. _____
2. _____
3. _____
4. _____
5. _____
6. _____
7. _____
8. _____
9. _____
10. _____
11. _____
12. _____
13. _____
14. _____

(over)

23. _____

_____

_____

_____

_____

_____

_____

23. _____

24. _____

25. _____

26. _____

27. _____

28. _____

29. _____

30. _____

31. _____

32. _____

33. _____

34. _____

35. _____

36. _____

37. _____

38. _____

39. _____

40. _____

Answer Tab
Lesson 29

NAME/DATE _____

1.
2.
3.
4.
5.
6.
7.
8.
9.
10.
11.
12.
13.
14.
15.
16.
17.
18.
19.
20.
21.
22.

(over)

Answer Tab
Practice Test 5

NAME/DATE _____

1.
2.
3.
4.
5.
6.
7.
8.
9.
10.
11.
12.
13.
14.
15.
16.
17.
18.
19.
20.
21.
22.

(over)

Answer Tab
Lesson 27

NAME/DATE _____

1.
2.
3.
4.
5.
6.
7.
8.
9.
10.
11.
12.
13.
14.
15.
16.
17.
18.
19.
20.
21.

Answer Tab
Lesson 28

NAME/DATE _____

1.
2.
3.
4.
5.
6.
7.
8.
9.
10.
11.
12.
13.
14.
15.
16.
17.
18.
19.
20.

29. _____ _____

30. _____ _____

NAME/DATE _____

(over)

1. _____
2. _____
3. _____
4. _____
5. _____
6. _____
7. _____
8. _____
9. _____
10. _____
11. _____
12. _____
13. _____
14. _____

15. _____
16. _____
17. _____
18. _____
19. _____
20. _____
21. _____
22. _____
23. _____
24. _____
25. _____
26. _____
27. _____
28. _____

NAME/DATE _____

1. _____
2. _____
3. _____
4. _____
5. _____
6. _____
7. _____
8. _____
9. _____
10. _____
11. _____
12. _____
13. _____

17. _____
18. _____
19. _____
20. _____
21. _____
22. _____
23. _____
24. _____
25. _____
26. _____

27. _____
28. _____
29. _____
30. _____
31. _____
32. _____
33. _____
34. _____
35. _____
36. _____
37. _____
38. _____
39. _____
40. _____

29. _____
30. _____
31. _____
32. _____
33. _____
34. _____
35. _____

Answer Tab
Lesson 24

NAME/DATE _____

8. _____
9. _____
10. _____
11. _____
12. _____
13. _____
14. _____
15. _____
16. _____

1. _____
2. _____
3. _____
4. _____
5. _____
6. _____
7. _____

(over)

Answer Tab
Lesson 25

NAME/DATE _____

20. _____
21. _____
22. _____
23. _____
24. _____
25. _____
26. _____
27. _____
28. _____

1. _____
2. _____
3. _____
4. _____
5. _____
6. _____
7. _____
8. _____
9. _____
10. _____
11. _____
12. _____
13. _____
14. _____
15. _____
16. _____
17. _____
18. _____
19. _____

(over)

29. ___
30. ___
31. ___
32. ___
33. ___
34. ___
35. ___
36. ___
37. ___
38. ___
39. ___
40. ___
41. ___
42. ___

13. ___
14. ___
15. ___
16. ___
17. ___
18. ___
19. ___
20. ___
21. ___
22. ___
23. ___
24. ___
25. ___

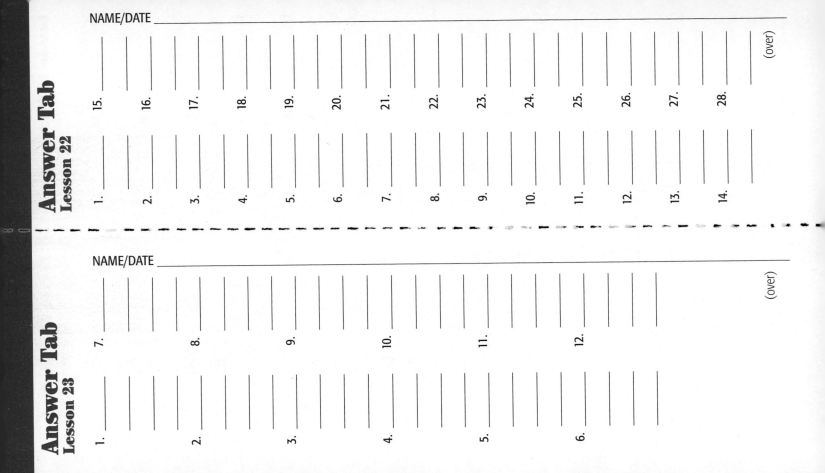

Answer Tab
Lesson 22

NAME/DATE _____

15. _____
16. _____
17. _____
18. _____
19. _____
20. _____
21. _____
22. _____
23. _____
24. _____
25. _____
26. _____
27. _____
28. _____

1. _____
2. _____
3. _____
4. _____
5. _____
6. _____
7. _____
8. _____
9. _____
10. _____
11. _____
12. _____
13. _____
14. _____

(over)

Answer Tab
Lesson 23

NAME/DATE _____

7. _____
8. _____
9. _____
10. _____
11. _____
12. _____

1. _____
2. _____
3. _____
4. _____
5. _____
6. _____

(over)

34. _____
35. _____
36. _____
37. _____
38. _____
39. _____
40. _____

41. _____
42. _____
43. _____
44. _____
45. _____
46. _____
47. _____
48. _____
49. _____
50. _____

33. _____
34. _____
35. _____
36. _____
37. _____
38. _____
39. _____
40. _____
41. _____
42. _____
53. _____

43. _____
44. _____
45. _____
46. _____
47. _____
48. _____
49. _____
50. _____
51. _____
52. _____

NAME/DATE _____

19. | _____
20. | _____
21. _____
22. _____
23. _____
24. _____
25. _____
26. _____
27. _____
28. _____
29. _____
30. _____
31. _____
32. _____
33. _____

(over)

1. _____
2. _____
3. _____
4. _____
5. _____
6. _____
7. _____
8. _____
9. _____
10. _____
11. _____
12. _____
13. _____
14. _____
15. _____
16. _____
17. _____
18. _____

NAME/DATE _____

19. _____
20. _____
21. _____
22. _____
23. _____
24. _____
25. _____
26. _____
27. _____
28. _____
29. _____
30. _____
31. _____
32. _____

(over)

1. _____
2. _____
3. _____
4. _____
5. _____
6. _____
7. _____
8. _____
9. _____
10. _____
11. _____
12. _____
13. _____
14. _____
15. _____
16. _____
17. _____
18. _____

57. _____

58. _____

59. _____

_____

_____

_____

54. _____

_____

55. _____

_____

_____

_____

_____

_____

56. _____

_____

_____

_____

Answer Tab
Lesson 19

NAME/DATE _____

1. _____
2. _____
3. _____
4. _____
5. _____
6. _____
7. _____
8. _____
9. _____
10. _____
11. _____
12. _____
13. _____
14. _____
15. _____
16. _____
17. _____
18. _____
19. _____
20. _____
21. _____
22. _____
23. _____
24. _____
25. _____
26. _____
27. _____
28. _____
29. _____
30. _____
31. _____
32. _____
33. _____
34. _____
35. _____
36. _____
37. _____
38. _____
39. _____
40. _____
41. _____
42. _____
43. _____
44. _____
45. _____
46. _____
47. _____
48. _____
49. _____
50. _____
51. _____
52. _____
53. _____
54. _____
55. _____
56. _____

(over)

Answer Tab
Lesson 20

NAME/DATE _____

1. _____
2. _____
3. _____
4. _____
5. _____
6. _____
7. _____
8. _____
9. _____
10. _____
11. _____
12. _____
13. _____
14. _____
15. _____
16. _____
17. _____
18. _____
19. _____
20. _____
21. _____
22. _____
23. _____
24. _____
25. _____
26. _____
27. _____
28. _____
29. _____
30. _____
31. _____
32. _____
33. _____
34. _____
35. _____
36. _____
37. _____
38. _____
39. _____
40. _____
41. _____
42. _____
43. _____
44. _____
45. _____
46. _____
47. _____
48. _____
49. _____
50. _____
51. _____
52. _____
53. _____

(over)

20. _____

21. _____

22. _____

23. _____

24. _____

25. _____

26. _____

27. _____

28. _____

29. _____

30. _____

40. _____

Answer Tab
Lesson 17

NAME/DATE _____

13.

14.

15.

16.

17.

18.

19.

(over)

1.

2.

3.

4.

5.

6.

7.

8.

9.

10.

11.

12.

Answer Tab
Lesson 18

NAME/DATE _____

20.

21.

22.

23.

24.

25.

26.

27.

28.

29.

30.

31.

32.

33.

34.

35.

36.

37.

38.

39.

(over)

1.

2.

3.

4.

5.

6.

7.

8.

9.

10.

11.

12.

13.

14.

15.

16.

17.

18.

19.

25. _____
26. _____
27. _____
28. _____
29. _____
30. _____
31. _____
32. _____
33. _____
34. _____
35. _____
36. _____

15. _____
16. _____
17. _____
18. _____
19. _____
20. _____

Answer Tab
Lesson 15

NAME/DATE _____

1.
2.
3.
4.
5.
6.
7.
8.
9.
10.
11.
12.
13.
14.
15.
16.
17.
18.
19.
20.
21.
22.
23.
24.

(over)

Answer Tab
Lesson 16

NAME/DATE _____

1.
2.
3.
4.
5.
6.
7.
8.
9.
10.
11.
12.
13.
14.

(over)

29. _____
30. _____
31. _____
32. _____
33. _____
34. _____
35. _____
36. _____
37. _____
38. _____
39. _____
40. _____
41. _____
42. _____
43. _____
44. _____
45. _____

44. _____
45. _____
46. _____
47. _____
48. _____
49. _____
50. _____
51. _____
52. _____
53. _____
54. _____
55. _____
56. _____
57. _____
58. _____
59. _____
60. _____
61. _____
62. _____
63. _____
64. _____
65. _____
66. _____
67. _____

Answer Tab
Lesson 13

NAME/DATE _____

1.
2.
3.
4.
5.
6.
7.
8.
9.
10.
11.
12.
13.
14.
15.
16.
17.
18.
19.
20.
21.
22.
23.
24.
25.
26.
27.
28.

(over)

Answer Tab
Lesson 14

NAME/DATE _____

29.
30.
31.
32.
33.
34.
35.
36.
37.
38.
39.
40.
41.
42.
43.

(over)

1.
2.
3.
4.
5.
6.
7.
8.
9.
10.
11.
12.
13.
14.
15.
16.
17.
18.
19.
20.
21.
22.
23.
24.
25.
26.
27.
28.